The Marketer's Visual Tool Kit

The Marketer's Visual Tool Kit

Terry Richey

American Management Association

New York • Atlanta • Boston • Chicago • Kansas City • San Francisco • Washington, D.C.
Brussels • Mexico City • Tokyo • Toronto

This publication is designed to provide accurate and authorita-
tive information in regard to the subject matter covered. It is sold
with the understanding that the publisher is not engaged in ren-
dering legal, accounting, or other professional service. If legal advice or other expert assistance is required, the services of a competent professional person should be sought.

Richey, Terry.
    The marketer's visual tool kit / Terry Richey
        p. cm.
    Includes bibliographical references and index.
    ISBN 0-8144-0213-5
    1. Marketing—Graphic methods.   I. Title.
HF5415.122.R53   1994
658.3—dc20   93-43007
                                                        CIP

Printing number

10 9 8 7 6 5 4 3 2 1

For Nancy, Sarah, Ben, and Tess

Contents

List of Illustrations

Acknowledgments

In the Introduction to *The Marketer's Visual Tool Kit*, I make a statement about business being a team sport. So is writing a book.

Nothing would have happened on this project without my fellow visual brainstormers at The Woods Group, Nancy Pope and Susan Odneal, who kept our business healthy, tested new visual tools, listened to my deadline complaints, and added ideas throughout the process.

Our company's outside board of directors (which I highly recommend having if you own a small, privately held company) supported the project with their usual good advice and ideas: Renny Arensberg, Ron Manka, Bob Priest, Humbert Tinsman, Jr., and Jim Tinsman.

The idea for *The Marketer's Visual Tool Kit* came as a recommendation from a wonderful change consultant, Marcia Manter, who proposed the idea as a way for our agency to utilize my systems as I moved from the advertising industry into marketing consulting.

Thanks also go to Jeff Herman, my literary agent, and to Adrienne Hickey of AMACOM for their enthusiastic support of the book.

Hundreds of business associates contributed to the book, although many without knowing it. I owe a debt of gratitude to all of The Woods Group's past and present clients and to our staff for tolerating me every time I picked up a felt-tip to doodle on a problem.

A number of Woods staff assisted on the project. They

include Janelle Smith, who drew the Cognitive Map; Charlene St. John; Jennifer Gustafson Hickerson; Kristen Sjoberg, who proofread (over and over); and Chris DeLong, who kept answering my questions as I tried to master several new graphics programs on my Mac.

This book uses numerous examples based on issues that I have been involved with for twenty years in my marketing business. All of the examples, however, are "invented" from experience and are not from actual companies or people.

Introduction: Working Together Visually

We're visual beings, but for some reason we forget that simple truth when we enter the business world. I've watched a product manager sweat out a three-page memo proposing a line extension when a simple, doodled chart would have done the job better. I've participated in planning meetings where everyone tries to reason through a marketing problem verbally, and after several hours of frustration, someone draws a crude flowchart that provides the solution.

Researchers are just beginning to unravel the mysterious power of visualization. New studies show that the mind has two classification systems, one language-based and one visually based,[1] each stored by a different part of the brain. By combining both the verbal and visual, we find maximum potential in communicating business issues.

You can use your natural visual skills to enhance your ability to think and communicate. Perhaps more important, visual solutions often build more solid consensus and teamwork. Working together to construct a Strategic Map or evaluate a Positioning Cube, your team will develop a common visual language that clarifies the exact meaning of the words you use.

My career allows me to spend an enormous amount of time watching successful business executives struggle with one of their most intimate concerns: thinking. I've watched the nimble thinker, the plodder, the fuzzy thinker, and the pretender. I've worked with bullies and copycats, clowns and academics. But watch most successful executives and you usually find a felt-tip pen, a big pad of paper, or a chalkboard close at hand. Whether by instinct or training, these executives know the power of the visual.

As you read this book, you'll find dozens of tools to bring your visual sense out of hiding and to enhance your business career. And maybe as important, you'll have fun doing it.

Each chapter offers visual solutions to the kinds of everyday marketing problems we all encounter. The book provides a selection of tools, not a comprehensive program. You will find ample ideas for common marketing dilemmas and a sense of how to use these tools in actual situations.

If your job touches on marketing in any way, visual tools offer a reliable weapon against confusion. This book will help you see a problem; it then will provide a real-life, step-by-step example of how a particular visual tool works in that situation. The bottom line for your time investment with this book will be that:

- You will think more quickly and clearly using visual tools.
- You will enhance your creativity when you think visually.
- You will present your ideas more persuasively when they are built on a visual foundation.
- You will achieve better teamwork and better results by creating visual models of your marketing issues and solutions.

In all of the scenarios and examples presented, no one works alone. Everyone works with a group to build agreements. That is quite intentional. These thirty visual tools can certainly help you clarify your thinking individually, but business is a team sport. Visual thinking performs its greatest service for a team.

In many of my consulting assignments, just one visual tool often becomes the focal point of our planning. That same visual is used over and over, modified year after year. You do not need an arsenal of visual tools to add significant value to your marketing efforts. One tool can sometimes do the job.

In our consulting practice, we also group a series of visual tools together into a customized system from which our clients can build their marketing strategies and tactics. This technique may be something you want to use after catching the visual planning bug.

You should also invent your own visual tools! Nothing works better for a particular problem than a tool you create just to solve it. The examples in this book can serve as a template to begin your exploration of visual thinking.

Copy these visual tools and use them directly out of this book. Modify them or make up your own to create your own tool kit. Once you get the visual power of communications working for you, new vistas of teamwork and problem solving will open up!

Note

1. A case study in *Nature* by two Johns Hopkins researchers reported how brain injury could destroy the "word" part of memory while the visual memory remained intact.

The Marketer's Visual Tool Kit

CHAPTER 1

▓

Do I Have to Draw You a Picture? Building Agreement on Marketing Issues

How many times have you sat through a meeting, thinking that everyone agreed on the issue and direction, only to find out later that several of the participants heard remarkably different issues and directions? I cherish words. But despite our care with them, in business their meaning and emphasis vary greatly. Not so with visual tools. Placing a point on a grid makes an eloquent statement in which the only disagreement is the exact placement of the point rather than the meaning of the words used.

You can use your natural visual skills to enhance your ability to think and communicate. And despite what you might believe, you do have natural visual skills. Have you ever planned a vacation? You visualized yourself skiing or lying on the beach. Have you ever drawn a map to your house? That map transferred a complex series of instructions visually.

Understanding that we really do think visually is the first step in unleashing this powerful communication tool. Our minds have an uncanny ability to store images and a severely limited ability to store words. Recall the poem you committed to memory in seventh grade, and then recall your classroom and school yard. Which came to mind more easily?

Why are we "naturally" visual? Because this is a book about business and not science, I'll float just three equally plausible reasons that I've come up with.

First, we're "closet" hunters. We've carried forward those instincts that our ancient relatives used to size up prey and then successfully acquire dinner. To shoot an arrow at a galloping bison required raw nerve and something else—visualization. The arrow had to be released well ahead of the target.

The second reason we are naturally visual is that we have the intelligence to be so. All creatures' nervous systems have the ability to "think." At its most basic level, this is just a reaction to a stimulus. But as the creature becomes more advanced, it can begin to anticipate a possible stimulus. Then, as it becomes *more* advanced, it plans alternatives to the stimulus. And finally, it controls the stimulus to get the desired outcome. Let's say you and I are playing chess. You move a pawn forward, then I select a countermove and visualize what your next likely move will be in response. A chess master is said to have the ability to think as far as six moves ahead. Our culture tends to attribute mastery of chess with intelligence. In fact, it is the enhanced ability to visualize that separates the masters from good chess players. Our desire to visualize creates the need for the game board and pieces in the first place.

The third reason, which is my favored reason, for why we are naturally visual is that it gives us pleasure. Pleasure is associated with our ability to conjure up favorite images. Sitting in the sweltering sun on a hot aluminum bleacher watching a slow-moving Little League game, you can cool off mentally by visualizing last year's mountain cabin and ski trip.

We also find pleasure in the control that visualization gives us. Working with clients on long-range planning, I find it a useful technique to develop a series of possible scenarios that represent how the future may unfold. Getting the group members to visualize what their company would be like in each of these scenarios provides them with a real sense of control. We may not like the conceivable future, but our ability to anticipate its possibility and plan a reaction provides a quiet sense of comfort, a feeling most of us find pleasurable.

Pencil Phobia

Why is it that when someone says he doesn't "get it," a flip response is, "Do I have to draw you a picture?" We instinctively know that the fastest way to communicate is visually. Yet we seldom make the effort because of pencil phobia! We're unwilling to pick up a pencil and draw.

Sometimes the reason is that we don't want to offend. Will our client think we are talking down to her, or will the boss suspect we think he needs a chart to follow the flow of our plan? Sometimes we want to seem more "professional" or "intellectual," although I've never seen a business proposal's success hinge on how professional or intellectual the presentation was. Few would argue that professionalism and good thinking are critical ingredients. Yet I've often seen average ideas take home the prize because the presenter was able to build a visual bridge to his prospect and use that bridge to transport all of the ideas that he so desperately wanted the prospect to accept.

We can use visual thinking to understand a problem. And we can use it to convey the essence of the problem to someone else so she can understand it the way we do.

Visual thinking can begin with the three basic shapes we all learned to draw before kindergarten: the triangle, the circle, and the square. The triangle encourages you to rank parts of a problem by priority. When drawn into a triangle, these parts are less likely to get out of order and take on more importance than they should. While the triangle ranks, the circle encloses and can be used to include and/or exclude. Some problems have to be enclosed to be managed. Finally, the square serves as a versatile problem-solving tool. By assigning it attributes along its sides or corners, we can suddenly give a vague issue a specific place to live and to move about.

Let's look at the three shapes in turn.

The Triangle

The triangle is one of the best tools for visualizing a problem. Every difficult problem I've encountered in business breaks down into pieces, which carry different weight and importance. The pieces with the most importance sit at the top of the triangle, which progresses down to the sometimes thorny but less important piece at the base.

When we consider all of the elements of a problem equally, there are too many conflicting "voices" to manage. We begin to lose our ability to prioritize, organize, and ultimately find solutions. The triangle helps us visually build consensus on the relative importance of each component and then build a solution on the right foundation. The following scenario gives an example of real pyramid power.

The GoodFood Company makes one of the best gourmet cat foods on the market. Sales and profits have increased year after year, until this quarter. The field sales force projects flat revenues and is strongly urging management to cut prices to respond to competition. The product manager recommends major advertising expenditures. The CEO wants to minimize new expenses or discounting, yet keep her cat food on a slow growth curve to support the costly introduction of a new dog food planned for next year. Everyone has a solution, and yet just what is the problem?

Rather than spend hours discussing the merits of the various proposed solutions, the CEO brought her key staff together and had them start to visualize as a group. She began the process by asking, "What is the problem?" Competitors are cutting prices, said the sales manager. Not enough visibility, said the product manager. We need better distribution and an 800 order line, said the marketing director. The packaging needs improvement, added the production manager. "Let's list these problems," the CEO said:

- Higher Pricing
- Lack of Visibility
- Poor Distribution
- No 800 Number
- Poor Packaging

"Let's put some priority to the problem of sales being flat right now," the CEO said, and she drew a triangle with five segments.

The staff agreed that the least immediate of these problems for the moment was packaging, because the company had a year's supply in inventory and another year's supply already canned. "Poor Packaging" thus moved to the bottom segment of the triangle.

Then, after much discussion, they agreed to put "Poor Distribution" just above packaging because they had the strongest rep groups in each market and up until this quarter had been pleased with the results. The problem should be looked at, but it was less immediate to the goal of improving sales right now. "Lack of Visibility" came next for many of the same reasons. "No 800 Number" followed, and the top segment of the triangle contained the pricing problem (see Figure 1-1).

* * * * *

What the CEO accomplished with her visual far surpassed what could have been accomplished in written documents. She created, with consensus, a visual picture of the key problems facing GoodFood and where the priority of everyone's efforts had to be to increase sales next quarter. The words of the meeting will fade in a few days—the visual won't. Sales are off. The priority issue is pricing. Now the company can explore some solutions.

The Circle

Circle the wagons. The winner's circle. Circle of friends. We use the idea of a circle to both include and

Figure 1-1. Using a triangle to prioritize.

exclude. Why not make it visual? That's why the circle is such a powerful business tool, especially for defining boundaries.

A common mistake in problem solving is to encompass too much territory, which dilutes any solution's chance of success. For example, a prospective client who developed software told me that his market was "everyone in the United States" because his product was so simple to use and universally needed. I asked if one needed a computer to use his product and he said yes. What kind of computer? It had to be an IBM or clone. What language was the manual written in? English.

So with just a few questions, it became obvious that his immediate market was not 250 million Americans but only the small percentage who used IBM-compatible computer equipment and spoke English. When we define a problem (or opportunity) too broadly, we open ourselves up to missing the simple and obvious solutions.

However, the opposite error occurs more frequently. If

we define a problem too narrowly, we may be fixing the noisy engine while the boat sinks.

A friend who owned a typesetting company viewed the rapid advances in desktop publishing with some alarm. He believed he provided a quality service and told everyone he knew, in sometimes colorful terms, how little he thought of computer graphics. When I suggested that he enlarge his definition of his business to encompass desktop publishing, he scoffed. Today, many of his clients have moved on to more flexible companies that service their desktop typesetting needs. Drawing the circle around just a part of the problem to be solved and not considering enlarging the circle when new data are available can be hazardous to the health of your marketing plan. Let's see how the circle was used in the following case.

Chuck, a stockbroker, said that he felt blessed that he lived in "interesting times." He had outlasted his third national brokerage firm, and he and his staff of three were moving to a fourth. The staff consisted of a young sales associate named Tracy and two administrative assistants.

Business had been turbulent during the past five years, and the broker had a diverse mix of clients and products. The young sales associate was getting restless doing introductory calls for the more experienced broker. As they got ready to move to the new firm, Chuck and Tracy agreed to take a few days off for planning time.

As they began their planning meeting, it became apparent that Tracy wanted more room to grow, and Chuck agreed to look at options. The problem seemed to be determining what their market was and how they could divide it more equitably. Chuck felt that the lines were clear. To demonstrate, he drew a group of circles to represent the current division and relative size of accounts, as shown in Figure 1-2.

Tracy didn't see the division of accounts as neatly defined as Chuck did. In fact, she sketched her own visual (see Figure

Figure 1-2. Chuck's view of the business.

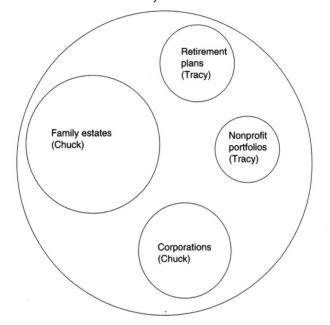

1-3) as she explained the problem. To Tracy, it appeared that Chuck's prospects often overlapped with hers, since many times a family estate was entwined in a retirement plan. Tracy felt the only area she had full responsibility for was the nonprofit institutions, a piece of business that Chuck was not interested in.

Chuck and Tracy moved more quickly to understanding each other's perceptions by the use of a visual. Tracy was handling the smaller accounts that overlapped Chuck's area of focus. Chuck didn't want to give up the smaller accounts, but he felt he couldn't service them personally. It became clear that the circles they had been working within did not have borders clear enough to reduce conflict. After much discussion, the brokers agreed to look at other ways to divide up their business, as illustrated in Figure 1-4.

With Chuck's long-term goal of maintaining a small but steady volume of high-income business and with Tracy starting into her portfolio-building years, a natural delineation for new prospects was based on their net worth. If it was under

Figure 1-3. *Tracy's view of the business.*

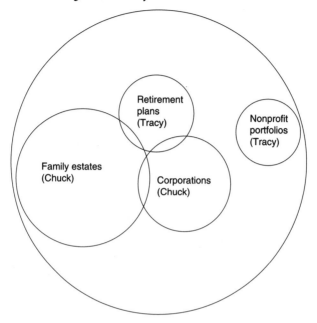

$1 million, Tracy got the prospect; if it was over $1 million, Chuck did. The new plan gave Tracy the opportunity to build large accounts over time and assured Chuck that he would not be working at cross-purposes with her.

The Square

The square has always had a no-nonsense sort of image. Stable, solid, and—well—square. Perhaps that's why it is the shape used in business visuals in those rare cases where a visual is even bothered with. Flip through most business books and you'll find precious few places for your eye to stop and your visual brain to engage. But when you do, the shape of the graphic, chart, matrix, table, or diagram is certainly square. It's a comfortable shape, which makes it a valuable implement in your kit of visual communication tools.

We can build business ideas out of squares. They can get more and more complex, transferring an enormous

Figure 1-4. Chuck and Tracy's shared view of their business.

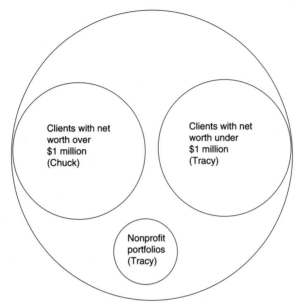

amount of data before anyone realizes what has happened. A square can combine some of the attributes of a triangle by ranking data or of a circle by defining a boundary. But it has some unique characteristics of its own, as shown in the following scenario.

EMARICO, a gift importer with a database of 12,000 customers, had been represented by a national sales organization for several years. To management's surprise, EMARICO's rep group dropped its lines in favor of a lower-priced competitor. Management began interviewing prospective representatives right away but felt that more immediate action was called for to prevent losing market share as a result of the changes. However, the company's limited marketing staff looked at contacting 12,000 customers as a daunting challenge. It was clear that the importer needed to act quickly and intelligently. The problem was how to separate the 12,000 customers into a number that was manageable for a small staff to deal with.

Figure 1-5. Customers divided by size and by how much they purchase.

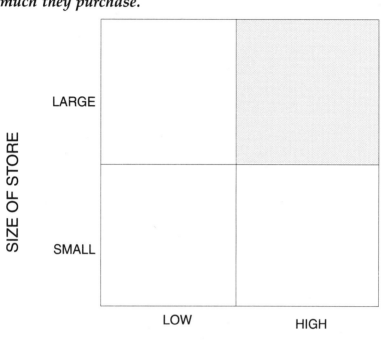

PURCHASES WITH EMARICO

The vice-president of sales drew up a quick plan and met with the CEO and other key executives. He divided a square into four equal segments and labeled them according to what he felt were the critical differences between EMARICO's customers. His view was that customers could be grouped by size and by how much they purchased from EMARICO (see Figure 1-5).

The vice-president's intention was to divide the database of 12,000 customers into the appropriate segments of the chart and then to concentrate efforts on the key segment (the shaded quadrant in Figure 1-5). By making a count from the database fields, he knew that the shaded area—customers that had large stores and were heavy purchasers of EMARICO products—totaled 1,800. That was a number he felt the marketing staff could manage.

Figure 1-6. Customers divided by new strategy.

	Segment A: 3,000 customers Large stores that do not buy much product from EMARICO. Future potential.	**Segment B:** 1,800 customers Large stores that buy high volume from EMARICO. Personal contact ASAP.
	Segment C: 3,700 customers Small stores that do not buy much product from EMARICO. Least important priority.	**Segment D:** 3,500 customers Small stores but high volume. Divide by number of years as customer with priority given to oldest.

SIZE OF STORE — LARGE / SMALL

LOW   HIGH

PURCHASES WITH EMARICO

But the CEO had other ideas. He looked at the squares and wondered if the company should be more concerned about small stores with high levels of orders because they had been more committed to EMARICO's lines and, once lost, would be hard to win back. Together, the president and vice-president formulated the strategy shown in Figure 1-6. The CEO and vice-president of sales agreed that all of Segment B and customers for over three years in Segment D would be their immediate priority, followed by the remainder of Segment D, then Segment A. Segment C would receive little effort until the new rep group was hired.

When the revamped squares were shown to the marketing team, it became immediately clear to them where the priorities were and why. And it became much easier to see when program implementation was getting off target from priorities.

Visualization with a tool like this simple square allows everyone to participate in understanding the problem more quickly. It serves as a translator between people with diverse backgrounds, motivations, and experiences.

* * * * *

A triangle. A circle. A square. Three simple shapes that can work hard to build understanding and agreement on marketing issues. If you are uncertain how to use them, ask yourself if the problem can be broken down into pieces of varying degrees of importance. If so, try a triangle. If it's a problem that centers around issues of what is included or excluded, draw some circles. And when you need to visualize various segments of the problem, choose a square.

But first of all, you have to pick up a pencil.

CHAPTER 2

■

A Surprise in Every Box:
Cultivating Innovation and Creativity

Imagination provides a remarkable fuel for driving the marketing process. For nearly twenty years in the creative side of advertising, I have seen imagination rescue many a dying company. And I have seen a lack of imagination erode the soul of even the most prestigious organizations. Innovation and creativity become the real product of most businesses with staying power.

Losing Your Creativity

No one sets out to be intentionally noncreative. Then why do so many of us succeed at wilting our imagination before it bears fruit? My experience leads me to believe it's because of three things. I call them the box, the clock, and the voice of judgment.

The Box

Much of my time now is spent working with management on long-range marketing planning. A common expression from this process is *working outside the box*. In any creative problem-solving situation, "the box" becomes those boundaries that limit your choice of solutions. At these planning sessions, someone inevitably suggests dropping the barriers and working outside the box. Then everyone gets quiet.

Very quiet.

When the box goes away, so does our ability to create. We need the foundation of boundaries to build new ideas. The goal is not to eliminate rules but to look at the rules from a different point of view. Creative geniuses do not get out of the box—they redefine the box in a new and insightful way.

If you want to inspire creative problem solving for you and your team, stay in a box, but make lots and lots of boxes. The visual tools in this chapter all work toward the goal of redefining the box.

The Clock

A national advertising and marketing company gives the "Showerhead Award" each month to the staff member who provides the most creative idea for its clients. Why a showerhead? The company understands where the really innovative ideas come from and how to encourage more of them.

We use the words *creative process* without thinking much about the "process" part. And there is a process. It starts with information gathering and absorption into the issue. I've found that the intensity of this first step affects the eventual creative result. The more absorbed and intense, the more creative. Through this intensity, you challenge all of the dimensions of the box your issue is in and study the rules so you can mold them later. This takes time and effort.

After the absorption process, most creative thinkers find their best ideas occur during a period of incubation in which they are not consciously trying to solve the problem. As your subconscious does its mysterious work, a creative solution springs forth at the most unlikely time and place, when you are not directly thinking about the problem. (Thus, the Showerhead Award for ideas that pop into your head in the shower.)

Absorption, intensity, and incubation take time—they cannot be rushed or scheduled. Trying to manage them within the confines of "the clock" surely leads to imagination frustration. Creativity pays no regard to time.

The Voice of Judgment

The third common barrier to real creativity speaks with a quiet little voice in your mind giving you all of the reasons why something will not work before you get it out of your head for a closer examination.

A sign in an ad agency's creative department reads BEWARE THE VOICE OF JUDGMENT. The creative staff knows that the most severe critic of their ideas is not the nervous agency account managers or the conservative client but the little voice in their own heads. All people are creative. But most people allow the voice of judgment to keep anyone else from knowing it.

The three visual tools you'll find in this chapter—the Cognitive Map, the Morpho Box, and the Opportunity Ladder—will assist you in stretching your imagination muscle and increasing your strength to wrestle with the box, the clock, and the voice of judgment.

Cognitive Mapping: A First Step Toward New Ideas

Many of us without the natural ability to draw yearn from time to time to be able to sketch. It's part of our built-in programming that tells us that drawing improves communication. Well, here's a technique that allows you to draw and communicate without any drawing skill! It's called Cognitive Mapping, and it's a visual assemblage of doodles, arrows, notes, and symbols that capture the process of solving a problem. And at the same time, it gives you a roadmap of how you arrived at the solution. Here's how it works.

Dyna Energy Corporation manufactures and markets industrial batteries. Its proprietary science gives it a group of products that enjoy long life and sustainable power, but at a premium price. Unfortunately, Dyna's largest client, a motorcycle manufacturer, just bought a competitive battery company and

Figure 2-1. The marketing director's Cognitive Map.

will be producing its product in-house. Dyna wants to build consensus on where to place its product development and marketing resources in light of this imminent loss of business.

The marketing director began the discussion by drawing on a large poster board a picture of how he saw the current situation (see Figure 2-1). In the several hours of discussion that followed, the planning team added, marked over, and modified the original drawing. And rather than redo the drawing with each change, the team allowed the sketch (Figure 2-2) to just evolve over time to reflect the group's shifting ideas. The visual collection of all of these ideas, whether dead ends or brilliant thoughts, is called a Cognitive Map. With the completed Cognitive Map, the marketing team from Dyna divided up responsibilities and moved ahead on their marketing program with a greater degree of confidence and consensus.

* * * * *

As the Dyna team learned, Cognitive Mapping has many benefits, such as the following:

- The group uses symbols in place of words to communicate more quickly and clearly the meaning of ideas.

Figure 2-2. The expanded Cognitive Map.

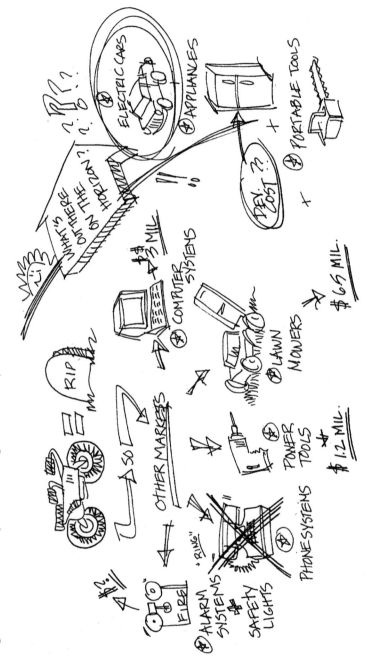

- The map limits the circular discussions in which old ground is revisited.
- It enhances creativity and innovation.
- It gives everyone an opportunity to participate.
- It produces a visual record of the meeting that can be reviewed later.
- It gives participants the satisfaction of shaping something tangible.
- It can indicate relative importance or emphasis.

Using a Morpho Box to Stretch the Rules

When really creative people work on a problem, they have the annoying tendency to forget the rules. They begin asking a lot of questions that suggest a lack of respect for "the way we've always done it" and "how our industry works." Creative people are eager to stretch the rules, and they have the ability then to sort and reassemble hundreds or even thousands of options to find a unique match that perfectly solves the problem. Yet most creative people remain unaware of just how the process works.

For those of us who would not define ourselves as highly creative, a wonderful visual tool, a Morpho Box, simulates the creative process and can lead to breakthrough marketing ideas.

The first step in using a Morpho Box requires that you clearly define the problem you are trying to solve. While this may seem apparent, don't take it for granted. If the problem is defined too broadly, you will remove all of the boundaries and will overdose on options. Next, array the key attributes of the product or service that relate to the problem along the top of a grid. Often, these can be "Who, What, When, Where, Why, and How," but they can also be various forms or functions of your product. A little experimentation is required to create the most useful box. Here's an example of how a Morpho Box actually works.

First United Bank operates eighty-seven branches in a densely populated coastal state. Each branch has an automated teller machine (ATM) on site, and the bank has another thirty ATMs at freestanding locations near bank branches. The bank's mindset has been to look at the ATM as a close-proximity substitute for a teller. The problem is that the machines are not being utilized enough to justify their cost. First United's marketing staff wants to take a look at the ATMs from a new perspective, and they use a Morpho Box as a tool to stretch their thinking.

Defining First United's problem too broadly could result in a vague mission such as "increase the bank's business." But too narrow a definition could prove equally hazardous—for instance, "increase the frequency of after-hour deposits." The art of creative problem solving lies in the care taken in defining the problem. In First United's case, the marketing staff began its search for ideas with a good problem definition: "How can we serve customers better using ATM equipment?"

The group began with a Morpho Box (Figure 2-3) and started their planning by listing across the top "What," "Where," "Why," "Who," "When," and "How." Over the next hour, they filled in each box below the category with an item that related to the use of an ATM. For example, under the "What" category, the group easily identified "Withdraw," "Deposit," "Get balance," and "Transfer." The machine provides those services now. The remaining empty boxes forced the group to stretch.

"I guess you could make payments of some sort," one team member suggested. Another suggested that if the keypad were enhanced, loan applications could be taken at the machine. And a third added that if you could apply for a loan, you should be able to select from an investment menu and transfer funds into investments.

While everyone in the group understood the pitfalls of several of these ideas (it's not how our industry works!), the leader kept the discussion open and freewheeling. Everyone agreed to suspend the "voice of judgment" during the idea-generation phase of the planning session.

Each category was filled in with the same process until the

Figure 2-3. Laying the foundation of the Morpho Box.

What	Where	Why	Who	When	How
Withdraw	Bank lobby	Speed			
Deposit	Drive-up	Privacy			
Get balance	Remote locations	After hours			
Transfer	Retail stores				
Make payment	Shopping centers				
Apply for loan	Airports/ hotels				
Invest	Computer modem	Apply	Retirees	On vacation	Open accounts

entire Morpho Box was complete. Then, the team leader pointed out that 700 combinations existed from the Morpho Box "menu." If just 1 percent were useful, the bank would have seven new ideas to work with in marketing its ATMs. So the group began looking at combinations. The most obvious ones jumped out. For example, the first line across the Morpho Box read: "Current customers could withdraw cash at night in the bank lobby with their ATM cards."

As the group progressed through the potential combinations, several new ideas began to surface—or perhaps they

Figure 2-4. Innovating with the completed Morpho Box.

What	Where	Why	Who	When	How
Withdraw	Bank lobby	Speed	Current customers	At night	With ATM card
Deposit	Drive-up	Privacy	Non-customers	Weekends	With password
Get balance	Remote locations	After hours	Travelers	Out of town	With credit card
Transfer	Retail stores	Save	Students	Business hours	With debit card
Make payment	Shopping centers	Leave message	Business-people	At work	With PIN
Apply for loan	Airports/ hotels	Get info	Children	In car	Linked accounts
Invest	Computer modem	Apply	Retirees	On vacation	Open accounts

were forced to the surface by the Morpho Box. An intriguing combination, highlighted in Figure 2-4, was: "Use the ATM to offer on-the-spot loan approval inside major retail stores by allowing people to apply for the loan using their credit cards to guarantee the purchase until the loan is processed." This would open up First United to large new markets of noncustomers. That intriguing combination got the group excited, and several other innovative ideas followed, involving use of the ATMs in locations convenient to large customer groups (such as the ballpark) and use of the machines in nontraditional ways.

*   *   *   *   *

The key to successful brainstorming lies in the team's willingness to suspend disbelief and experiment with new ways of looking at opportunities—something that can be done with a Morpho Box. At this point, concentrating on only the positive possibilities without reference to the inherent problems makes the process work.

Stepping Onto the Opportunity Ladder

"A beginning is the time for taking the most delicate care that the balances are correct." Frank Herbert begins his highly creative epic *Dune* with this admonition. His advice carries much meaning for creative problem solving. Selecting the "wrong" problem stifles creativity. If you want to be more innovative, you must take delicate care at the beginning.

Let's take a look at the anatomy of a problem to see the forces at play that stifle innovation. A helpful tool for that is an Opportunity Ladder. With it, we can visually plot how we are defining the problem and uncover larger issues (up the ladder) that may require solutions or smaller issues (down the ladder) that may be easier to solve.

Shelby Foods makes five superpremium soups offered in 10- and 16-ounce cans. The soup's prices are nearly double those of traditional competitors, but Shelby's quality and regional appeal provide it with good volume and margins. However, the last two quarters, adjusting for seasonality, show a disturbing falloff in sales for the 16-ounce size. And that creates a problem to solve.

Shelby's marketing staff began with the apparent problem at hand: "Sales on our 16-ounce cans are falling." Without taking care of beginnings, that could be the end of the problem definition and the group would begin to develop ideas and solutions to this apparent problem. And that could potentially worsen the *real* problem.

To define the real problem, the staff used an Opportunity Ladder to ensure that attention be placed on solving the right issue. The ladder shows two opposing forces. The pressure for immediate results pushes the problem identification down the ladder to more tightly restricted definitions. The pressure for greater future opportunities pushes problem identification up the ladder to broader definitions. Let's put Shelby's current problem near the middle of the ladder (see Figure 2-5) to find out what happens in an actual situation.

Shelby's team could develop solutions for the problem identified. Based on their definition, these solutions would focus on getting sales volume of the 16-ounce can to return to previous levels.

However, the more pressure for immediate results, the more likely the group will move down the Opportunity Ladder to an even more limited problem definition. One team member suggested the problem was that discount retailers were cutting orders, to which solutions such as cutting prices were suggested. Another member identified the problem as sales staff not pushing the 16-ounce size. Perhaps, she thought, adding some incentives on that size would get the orders back up.

But Shelby has an insightful marketing vice-president. He drew an Opportunity Ladder on the marker board and added in the problems identified so far.

Vice-president: We want to take care in defining our problem so we are not back here in a few quarters with the same problem and less time and fewer resources to fix it. We've taken the problem definition downstream, and I think we all feel comfortable that we can create solutions that will solve any of the problems we have identified. But is there a bigger problem out there?

Product manager: I was just wondering if we're finally getting some feedback from the market about our can size. Maybe

Figure 2-5. Placing a problem on the Opportunity Ladder.

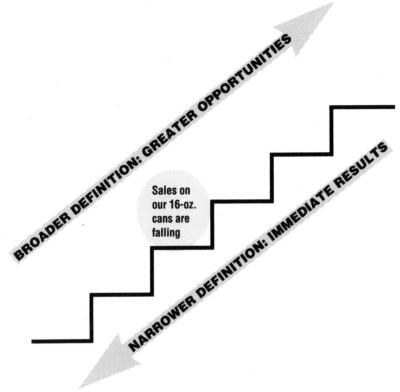

people want smaller sizes. It's been a factor for lots of other food manufacturers.

Vice-president: Good point. Let's get that down. If that were the problem, it would open up a whole bunch of issues about equipment, packaging, . . . even shelf space. Before we start to look at those, could there be any larger problem we should look at?

Sales manager: I don't think it's the size as much as the fact that families are smaller and you can't store the soup easily. If we could provide a plastic lid for storage, we could keep selling the same size.

Vice-president: I think you've hit on a couple of issues. We

Figure 2-6. Extending the problem up and down the Opportunity Ladder.

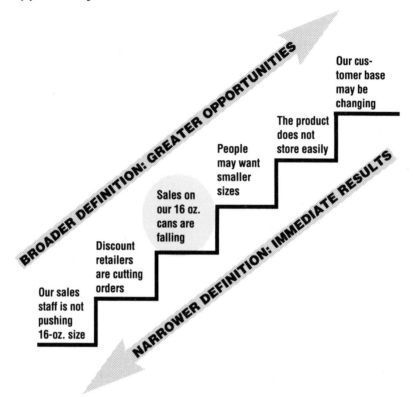

can certainly identify storage as a potential problem. Let's get it down here on our diagram. But you mentioned that families are smaller. We've never really looked hard at the demographics of our customers because our sales have been consistent, and frankly, we've felt locked in to our current sizes by the plant equipment. Could there be a larger problem such as that our customer base may be changing?

Product manager: I have some studies that may help us with that. And last week, I was talking with a Lipton product manager I met at the packaging conference and she suggested that we talk about swapping some production since they don't have a 16-ounce line. You know, another idea. . . .

At the end of the discussion, the Opportunity Ladder looked like the one shown in Figure 2-6.

* * * * *

That's the way problem definition works. You define too narrowly or in too much of a hurry and you may solve the problem at hand but miss the bigger opportunities. Great innovation needs great challenges. Beginnings take the most delicate care.

CHAPTER 3

![]

The Operation Was a Success, But . . . Creating a Winning Strategy

Strategy and tactics. Thinking and doing. Vision and execution. Whatever you call it, finding a balance between these two powerful forces of success remains a lifelong search for the best in any field: military leader, artist, baseball coach, or marketing manager.

But business fosters a particular fondness for tactics. That emphasis can lead to an imbalance that reduces the opportunities for success. We get so wrapped up in tactics—doing things to meet a quota or deadline, executing someone else's orders—that we miss the reason behind the tactics. Eventually the purpose of the tactic fades away, but the rules, quotas, deadlines, forms, and frustration remain.

What makes business so tactic-bound? If it's an entrepreneurial business, tactical skill may be what made the business grow in the first place. The entrepreneur, if nothing else, is a doer—trying this and that, learning by experimenting. The company naturally reflects the entrepreneur's style.

On the other hand, tactic mentality flourishes in mature businesses too. Traditionally, career success in these businesses has meant following the rules. Someone far up the food chain decides what needs to happen, and everyone else implements "the plan."

Remarkably, business is changing. The move to empower workers is really an acknowledgment that they have a stake in strategy as well as tactics, in thinking as well as doing.

Building a Strategic Map

One of the issues involved in moving strategy making down into the business organization concerns common understanding or focus. To carry out tactics, we do not need to share common objectives. But with strategy, we must interpret conditions, events, and actions in a similar manner to have any hope of creating a successful plan.

One proven way to share a common understanding of your market and your position in it is to create a Strategic Map. You build the map by searching for the two most critical variables that separate how you and your competitors differ and then plotting these variables in a box divided into quadrants. Building a Strategic Map of your business and creating consensus on the accuracy of that model can dramatically enhance the process of defining strategy and constructing results-driven marketing programs. The visual nature of your model keeps it top of mind and in clearer focus than words on paper can do alone. Let's see how a radio station used a Strategic Map in its efforts to create a winning strategy.

KDRY-AM, the "Voice of the Desert," has flourished as a broadcasting pioneer in a southwestern city of nearly 500,000 residents. But times have changed, and so has the competition. The growing success of FM stations, changing listening habits, CD-quality sound, and new developments in satellite feeds for national programming have reduced the once powerful voice of KDRY. Twenty years ago, the station had three competitors and a market share of 60 percent. Today, twelve stations cover its market, and the latest ratings give KDRY only an 8 percent share.

KDRY's owner realizes that he must cut overhead to stay

profitable, find a strategy to gain market share and revenue, or both. The problem: Everyone on the four-person management team has a different solution. Planning sessions over the past several months have ended in misunderstanding and inaction, with managers protecting their individual areas. Proposed solutions each garnered opposition:

Station manager:	Wants to lower costs by reducing live broadcasting during parts of the day and by picking up satellite feeds of national programming. *Strongly opposed by the programming director and marketing director, who fear lowering of quality.*
Programming director:	Wants to improve ratings by bringing in better, but more expensive, on-air talent for drive time. *Strongly opposed by the station manager, who does not want to add to the overhead, and the sales manager, who suspects it will lead to more expensive spots to sell.*
Sales manager:	Wants to become more competitive in pricing and (he hopes) to increase revenue by lowering rates through package deals. *Strongly opposed by everyone else for its possible impact on short-term revenue.*
Marketing director:	Wants to change to a nationally syndicated talk-radio format because no one in the city offers this. *Strongly opposed by the programming director and sales manager because of KDRY's tradition of local programming mixed with country music. Opposed by the station manager because of the uncertainty a new format might bring.*

The owner sensed gridlock among his team partly because each member preferred to make tactical decisions in his area of expertise rather than focus on strategic decisions that would set the station on a successful path. After weeks of haggling, the owner and the management team agreed to build a visual model—a Strategic Map—of their business. They started by answering the question: What are the key issues that separate how KDRY and competitive stations operate?

In surprisingly short order, they arrived at two issues: (1) how much importance the station placed on programming, particularly local programming, and (2) how promotional the station was in selling advertising. In the big picture, the group decided that the differences among stations were how each allocated resources to serve either listeners or advertisers.

To start the Strategic Map, the owner drew a simple box divided into four quadrants. Along the horizontal side, he wrote "Programming Focus," with "Low" on the left and "High" on the right. Then vertically, he wrote "Advertising Focus," with "Low" on the bottom and "High" on the top. Each of the four quadrants, as a result of the different combination of characteristics, identified a different type of station. The management team agreed that the graph, shown in Figure 3-1, represented a simplistic but accurate way to map their competitive environment.

The owner asked the group to discuss the qualities found in each quadrant. Stations ranked low on programming focus and high on advertising focus (Quadrant I) would likely run numerous promotions, cut ad rates when it would serve an advantage, and offer a variety of other incentives to advertisers. At the same time, these stations would not put their resources into having the best on-air talent, would reduce costs by airing national programming, and would offer only limited local news. The team agreed to call these competitors "Promotional Stations," and agreed that these are quite often the stations with out-of-town owners.

Contrasted with that, Quadrant IV holds stations with a strong commitment to local programming, perhaps even of a specialized nature. These stations are not as aggressive in courting advertisers. They have a mission to get their message out, not to increase revenues to their highest levels. The team dubbed these "Special Interest Stations" and used as examples the local public radio station affiliated with the university and the local religious station.

Quadrant III holds those stations that neither take an aggressive approach to finding advertisers nor have a high commitment to local community programming. These "Utility

Figure 3-1. The beginnings of a Strategic Map.

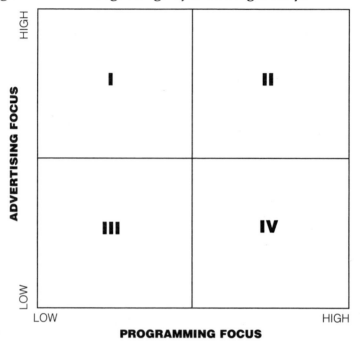

Stations" have found a niche by cutting overhead to a minimum. In fact, many of these stations are automated during the day and do not broadcast at night. Much of their programming comes through national syndication. Sales staff is lean and limits the opportunity to develop any special deals.

Finally, in Quadrant II, stations provide significant community involvement along with quality local programming and a highly aggressive approach to promotions and advertising. These "Traditional Stations" are the high-overhead, high-profile community information leaders.

With the Strategic Map visualized to this extent (see Figure 3-2), the owner moved on to the next step. He asked the group to locate KDRY and each of the eleven competitive stations within the quadrants. After an hour of interesting discussion, the Strategic Map looked like the one shown in Figure 3-3.

That part of the plan completed, the owner reviewed the team's accomplishments:

Figure 3-2. The Strategic Map with the quadrants defined.

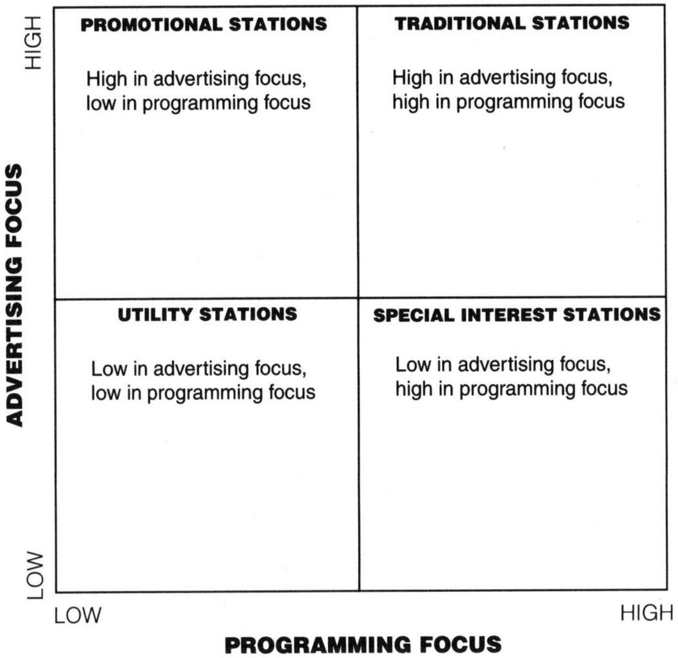

	PROMOTIONAL STATIONS	TRADITIONAL STATIONS
	High in advertising focus, low in programming focus	High in advertising focus, high in programming focus
	UTILITY STATIONS	SPECIAL INTEREST STATIONS
	Low in advertising focus, low in programming focus	Low in advertising focus, high in programming focus

(Vertical axis: ADVERTISING FOCUS, from LOW to HIGH. Horizontal axis: PROGRAMMING FOCUS, from LOW to HIGH.)

- The team reached agreement that two key strategic differences existed between stations.
- The team agreed that stations fell within the four combinations (quadrants) of these two issues.
- The team agreed on where KDRY and its competitors were located on the Strategic Map.

*   *   *   *   *

Now that the group had at least developed consensus on definitions, the owner told the team what he believed and how they should proceed:

> We're all here because we want our station to succeed. But before we go further in this planning process, I want to make a few comments so that you know what my agenda is and how

Figure 3-3. The Strategic Map with the twelve stations positioned.

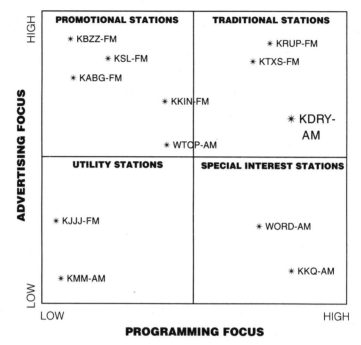

I feel. First of all, I want to operate a profitable radio station, one that gives me and the staff a good return for our effort. It doesn't matter to me which of the quadrants KDRY is in, but whichever it is, I want it to be the best in our niche.

It's not "bad strategy" to be a Utility Station. But it is bad strategy to try to be a Utility Station one month and a Traditional Station the next. I believe there is an optimal strategy for each different quadrant, and not working the optimal strategy will lead to problems. Let's shade the area of each quadrant that would be the optimal zone for each. Assume that the higher on either programming or advertising focus, the greater will be the cost.

The team began discussing the relative merits of spending their resources in each quadrant. They started with the Promotional Stations. And after much discussion, they agreed that the station that would do the best in this quadrant would put most of its resources into advertising, whether special promotions, discounts and rate cuts, or more sales staff. The station would offer enough programming quality to be competitive in its quadrant but place most resources into advertising programs.

The team then shaded in the Promotional Station quadrant's optimal zone—the area where spending resources would produce the most successful station. The team spent their resources on the advertising side of the quadrant to ensure that they would have a competitive advantage. And while they felt that the best Promotional Station focused on advertisers, they did not believe that the best strategy would let that factor completely dominate. So they moved the optimal zone down slightly from the highest level of advertising focus, as shown in Figure 3-4.

The team then developed similar optimal zones for the other three quadrants. For Traditional Stations, the optimal zone needed to balance the interests of advertisers with those of listeners. And since providing the best in both appeared cost-prohibitive, the group's shaded area for most success fell toward the central area of the quadrant.

The team decided that Utility Stations have yet a different optimal zone. The objective: to reach the lowest level of expense that will maintain a small but stable market share. And while stations in this quadrant have lower expenses both for ad promotions and program-

Figure 3-4. The optimal zone in the Promotional Stations quadrant.

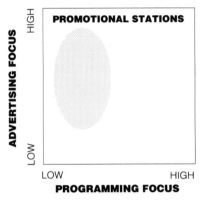

ming, the group felt the most successful strategy would emphasize the advertiser over the listener.

Finally, the Special Interest Stations must, of necessity, emphasize programming to hold their audiences. Since most of these stations rely on donations or income other than from advertisers, the shaded area shifted to low on the advertising scale. After creating the optimal zones in each quadrant, the Strategic Map looked like the one shown in Figure 3-5.

The team then spent some time discussing why some of the stations, including theirs, were operating outside of the optimal zones and what consequences came with that positioning. The Strategic Map had created some insights that the group had overlooked in their previous planning sessions. The owner moved ahead to describe another use of the Strategic Map:

> I've had a feeling that part of our inability to develop a plan for how to get the station back on a profitable track is that we have not had agreement on where we are and where we are headed. Our map has helped. It's clear that we are out of the optimal zone and that we need to

Figure 3-5. The completed Strategic Map.

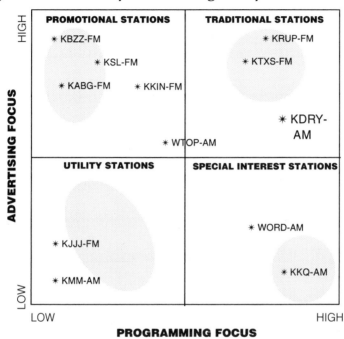

make adjustments to get closer to it as soon as possible. Let's take a look at some of the tactics each of you suggested in light of our map.

Improving our programming by adding better drive-time talent clearly would move us further away from the optimal zone. But a more promotional approach to packaging ad sales takes us in the right direction. That's assuming we want to stay in the Traditional Stations quadrant. Any thoughts?

Looking at the completed Strategic Map, the team saw that opportunities in the optimal zone of the Promotional Stations quadrant were limited because of intense competition. The Special Interest Stations quadrant would not hold enough profit potential to move into. But

Figure 3-6. Potential marketing changes and their directions on the Strategic Map.

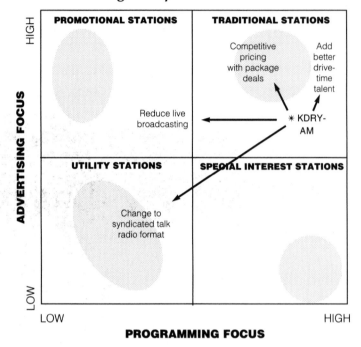

a vigorous discussion developed on the wide-open opportunities of the Utility Stations quadrant. After several more hours of work, a group of possible directions was established from Strategic Mapping (see Figure 3-6):

- KDRY-AM would become more promotional in its pricing to move into the optimal zone of the Traditional Stations quadrant.
- The management team would make inquiries into buying one of the stations now operating outside of an optimal zone with plans to convert it to a syndicated talk radio Utility Station, taking advantage of that apparent opportunity.
- The team would update the Strategic Map each quarter at the group's management meeting.

Growing a Decision Tree

To plan useful strategy, you must take a hard, honest look at your product or business as well as at your competition. The Strategic Map can help you do that. But you cannot freeze your business environment, which is constantly being reshaped by outside driving forces. Marketing managers must track changing consumer demands and shifting competitors' strategies. Successful strategy development can be enhanced by visual tools that show a range of options in graphic form. One of the simplest and most valuable is a Decision Tree.

The key to strategy is the ability to think forward and reason backward. We imagine where the future will take us and then build a pathway back to today. The problem lies in not knowing which of many possible futures will unfold. A Decision Tree allows you to visualize these futures and evaluate their potential impact from the future, rather than from today. Here's how one company used a Decision Tree.

UVu Video operates a chain of thirty-six company-owned video stores in fourteen Pacific Coast cities. Each year for the past five years, the revenue of UVu has tripled. The two partners work long hours to keep up with growth far beyond their expectations. The more aggressive of the partners has developed a plan to open another twenty stores within the next five years. Based on current operations and UVu's obvious ability to pick good locations, the company's bankers are encouraging the expansion.

However, the conservative partner has grown increasingly worried about the threat of new technologies. At some point in the future, cable or telephone companies will deliver specific movies at specific times with the ease of a phone call. Will people continue to use video stores when they have a more convenient and perhaps less expensive option to see movies?

Discussions between the partners have grown heated over

Figure 3-7. Three primary strategies plotted on the Decision Tree.

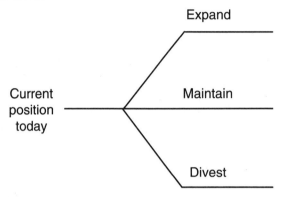

the expansion plan. Each conversation seems to end in a confusion of "what ifs." To sort out how the future might unfold (think ahead) and how they should react now (reason backward), the partners drafted a Decision Tree. They looked ten years ahead and considered what might happen to UVu (and them) with three possible futures: (1) a declining industry, (2) a steady industry, and (3) a booming industry. Here's how their Decision Tree grew.

UVu has three primary strategies: to expand, maintain, or divest, as shown in Figure 3-7. Different futures call for different strategies, but no one knows which future will unfold. By moving further down the Decision Tree branches, relative risk and reward can be assessed to eliminate some options that would not be worth pursuing under any market condition.

The partners took one option, to divest or contract the size of the business, and arranged the available options. Along this branch, they could see situations advantageous to franchising their current stores (and sharing the potential risk and reward with other investors), diversifying into other businesses (and diluting the risk they face with the video stores), or selling their business. The Decision Tree's new branches are shown in Figure 3-8.

On the original branch labeled "Maintain," the partners did not see any significant alternatives, so they extended that Decision Tree line rather than branching it off.

Figure 3-8. Expanding the branches of the Decision Tree.

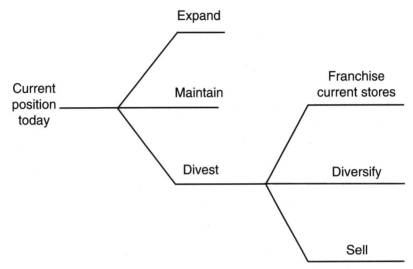

Finally, they tackled the choice of expanding the UVu business. Here they saw only two primary alternatives: (1) to own the new expansion stores under the same program that they have with the current group of thirty-six stores, or (2) to franchise most or all of the new expansion stores to distribute risk to other investors. (They recognized that they would also reduce their potential reward at the same time.)

With Figure 3-9, the visual display of the major choices facing UVu Video, the partners faced a decision. Often, just the process of physically graphing these options leads to a conclusion obscured before a pencil was put to it. But not this time. The partners still faced the dilemma that they have different views of the future. And while both expressed a good deal of uncertainty about their prospects, one partner believed that the party could go on for at least another ten years. The other worried about losing what they had spent years of hard work to build. So they tackled the problem by going one step further.

With the Decision Tree taken out to this point, the partners added a chart that would evaluate the range of possibility for the future, from +10, representing maximum growth and in-

Figure 3-9. Further growth of the Decision Tree branches.

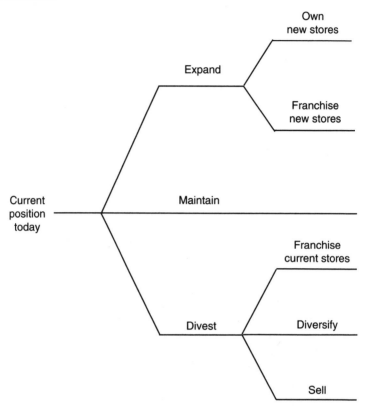

come, to −10, representing bankruptcy. They used this rating system to evaluate the three simplified futures of the video business: It may decline, it may remain steady, or it may boom. The key question was: How will we fare in the three different futures depending on which branch we choose from the Decision Tree? They took their time making these evaluations, and each did some compromising. In the end, they had Figure 3-10, a Decision Tree with an assessment of how positive or negative each outcome might be.

The Decision Tree allowed the partners to take some of the emotion out of the process of identifying possible future options. The tree did this because it provided an examination of

Figure 3-10. Weighing the possible outcomes for each choice on the Decision Tree.

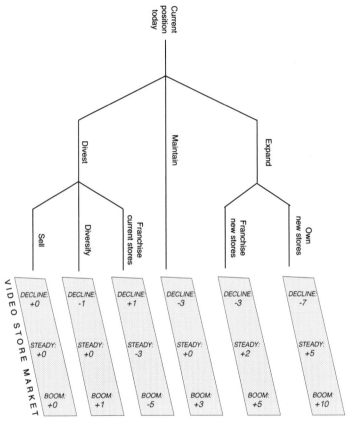

multiple futures and the range of possibilities within them rather than a discussion of just one or two.

With a clearer understanding of options, risks, and rewards, the partners more easily came to an accommodating resolution of their dilemma. The more conservative partner realized, with the aid of the Decision Tree, that the upside in either the Divest or Maintain branch would not satisfy him. And he also realized that his fear of the downside was somewhat exaggerated. Meanwhile, the Decision Tree did not slow the more aggressive partner's interest in expanding. So they reached a compromise. They would expand, but only by franchising. The aggressive partner will purchase franchises herself to participate more fully in what she sees as a booming opportunity. The other partner will benefit more conservatively from the expansion, but he will be allowed to maintain his comfort zone with the investment. By thinking ahead and reasoning backward, the partners found a course that could satisfy both of them.

*   *   *   *   *

On the landing gear lever of the newest high-tech jetliner, a miniature wheel spins at the end of the handle. Its only purpose: to instantly convey what the lever does. Despite all of the pilot training and computer sophistication, the little wheel remains the ultimate communication tool because it is visual, tactile, and real. That's the advantage of putting strategic issues in visual form. Decision makers can share a context for defining current conditions and future choices. And the visual model created will live long in your memory.

CHAPTER 4

![image]

Second Might as Well Be Last:
Evaluating Your Product

In marketing, only one certainly, fatal decision exists: Become the second company to introduce a product or service not clearly better, faster, cheaper, or more reliable than the first company's. So days, months, and sometimes years are spent studying a product and why its features are better than the competition's. Ultimately (and in a surprisingly short time) the customers decide, on their own, if you offer something better. Customers can be imaginative, smart, and quite cruel.

Take, for example, Avon's product Skin So Soft.® Although it was created as a bath oil, customers have discovered an array of unrelated uses for it, from removing scuff marks on floors to repelling insects. Despite all of the care Avon took in developing, positioning, and marketing the product, Avon's customers had needs that the marketing staff had not seen. Skin So Soft met those needs, and today it's one of Avon's best-selling products.

Customers are intelligent, as the following story shows. A large regional hospital decided to package all of its programs and services that pertained to women and to develop a Women's Center. Research showed that women in the marketing area had a genuine interest in programs that made their lives easier and saved them money. Eighteen program features emerged, ranging from sick child day care to free admission for health screenings to a $500 discount on hospital admissions.

The hospital planned to provide all of these benefits for a small fee to women joining the Women's Center.

In further research, women ranked the eighteen features in order of importance. Four of the features led the study. While it was rarely ranked first, the $500 discount on hospital admissions nearly always showed up in the top three features selected. Just before launching a $250,000 promotion for the Women's Center, hospital executives reduced the discount to $100, with the rationale that this feature was not ranked number one in the research study.

After three months of intensive advertising and promotional effort, the new Women's Center had only 143 members. The hospital had budgeted for 2,500. Based on ad expenditures, acquiring each new member had cost nearly $1,750, rather than the $100 the hospital had expected, based on meeting original projections. Potential customers proved smarter than the marketers. They looked at the total package of features and made an evaluation based on that entire package. Reducing the discount had a profound impact that the hospital executives did not anticipate. In their manipulation of spreadsheets, they had lost touch with what women really wanted.

And customers can be cruel. Just as soon as you develop a new product or service, someone else will begin to modify it and make it better. McDonald's did not create the first hamburger. IBM did not invent the computer. The only way to stay on top is to keep watch with one eye on your product's features and their enhancement and the other eye on how customer needs are changing.

Features of a product or service become critical to its ultimate success. Careers are made or damaged by choosing the right features for a product. It's in this highly charged environment that visual marketing can give you a significant boost. Visual tools allow you to distill the right features to promote, to understand the benefit behind the feature, to look for new ways to market the product, and to understand where a product fits into the marketing life cycle.

Building Your Case: The FAB Grid

"Our computer security product is the only one with the XP-335 Polarity Activated Sensor," the new marketing director of the new software company explained to me before our company was to develop a new sales brochure and video. Sounded good to me, so I asked just what the chip did. "Starts faster," he clarified. The product gave PC users a way to lock files on their hard drives and to provide several levels of increasingly sophisticated security. A late entry into the market, the product desperately needed a feature to make it clearly better than the competition.

Starting faster seemed to be the advantage. So how much faster did it start? "Eight times faster than our closest competitor," he beamed. I could see dramatic headlines before my eyes. And then the marketing director added with pride, "Our software starts 3/1000ths of a second faster than anyone else's."

Who cares about 3/1000ths of a second? How would you ever know, anyway? Where's the benefit? All of the people at the company had such pride in the technical advance of their XP-335 that they'd lost sight of its meaningless "benefit" to the customer.

One of the traditional ways to sort out the core value of product features is with a FAB (Feature/Advantage/Benefit) Grid. Placing features in this format helps force us to examine each feature for its advantage and ultimate benefit. In the FAB Grid, features are the attributes of the product: size, color, price, speed, special ingredients. Advantages are what the features do: small size, for example, that allows you to put the product in your purse. Benefits are the human need that the product's

Figure 4-1. Placing features in a FAB Grid.

FEATURE	ADVANTAGE	BENEFIT
ACCURACY		
COMPUTERIZATION		
SPEED		
MODERATE COST		
CPA REVIEW		
DISCOUNT ON PERSONAL TAX WORK		

feature fulfills: With one in your purse, you'll never face the embarrassing problem of . . . Let's see how using a FAB Grid helped one accounting firm.

NumberOne, Inc., an accounting firm, decided to offer small companies (ten to fifty employees) a specialized accounting service for their retirement plans. NumberOne's partners believed that their clients' CEO and controller were the decision makers for selecting a record keeper for their plans.

The partners at NumberOne developed a list of six features that they believed would appeal to their prospects. They put these features into a FAB Grid, as shown in Figure 4-1. Some of the partners favored different features as being the most important to explain to prospects. For example, the computer-oriented partner was proud of his department's leading-edge use of accounting software ("Computerization" on the FAB

Figure 4-2. The completed FAB Grid.

FEATURE	ADVANTAGE	BENEFIT
ACCURACY	Saves returning paperwork for corrections	Your company will look more competent
COMPUTERIZATION	Uses state-of-the-art software	??????????
SPEED	Gets reports out on a timely basis	Your employees will be happier with you and your company
MODERATE COST	Is a fair price	??????????
CPA REVIEW	Tax pros look over all work on your account	You'll worry less knowing experts have checked all work
DISCOUNT ON PERSONAL TAX WORK	Gives your employees some extra savings	You'll be appreciated for providing good, special benefits

Grid) and wanted to portray that as most important. Other partners preferred different features for emphasis.

All agreed to complete the FAB Grid together. After finishing the grid (see Figure 4-2), along with several hours of bantering arguments back and forth, the partners finally focused on what the real benefits were for the features that appeared strongest. The grid exposed the truth of the weak features, indicating that some had no apparent benefits. The act of charting each of the features to its logical benefit enabled the entire group to better put themselves in the minds of their prospective customers.

Plotting a Course: The Feature Spectrum

Now that the partners of NumberOne, Inc., have a clearer understanding of what the features are for their new service, another visual tool, a Feature Spectrum, can

Figure 4-3. Placing the first feature in the Feature Spectrum.

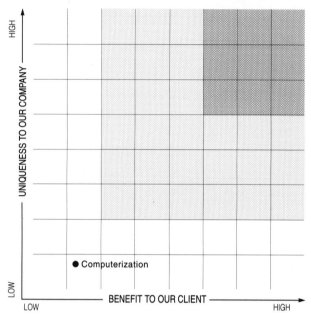

focus precisely on the issues selected for emphasis. The spectrum works by ranking the two conditions essential to evaluate product features for successful marketing: (1) How much does the feature benefit the client? (2) How unique is the feature to our product? Let's see what happened when a Feature Spectrum was used at NumberOne.

NumberOne's partners agreed that the computerization feature, under closer examination, had little benefit to the client. It made life easier for the accounting staff, but it might even appear as a negative to some clients who have an anticomputer bias. Computerization would thus rank low on the benefit scale. In a Feature Spectrum, we put this benefit scale across the bottom of a grid, with labels marking one side as "Low" and the other as "High" (see Figure 4-3).

Then vertically, we add another scale in which we rank

Figure 4-4. The completed Feature Spectrum.

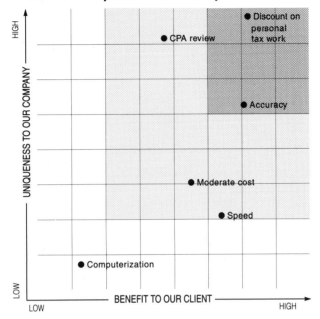

uniqueness from low to high. Computerization would also rank low on the uniqueness scale because most record-keeping services are computerized. At the point where both horizontal (benefit) and vertical (uniqueness) scales intersect, a mark is placed and labeled with that feature.

When the group members began to work on the Feature Spectrum, they placed each feature on both the benefit and uniqueness scales. As discussion progressed, the position of these points moved by consensus of the group. Eventually, all of the features were placed in the spectrum. The most important features were placed in the upper right corner of the spectrum, ranking high in both uniqueness and benefit. The least important features were placed in the lower left corner (see Figure 4-4).

*   *   *   *   *

The Feature Spectrum brings the right marketing thought process quickly into play. And it's one of the surest ways to build consensus on direction.

Figure 4-5. The Product Triad.

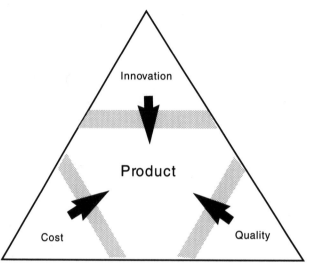

Pulling for Benefits: The Product Triad

Charged with the opportunity to develop a new product or change the course of an old one? Get ready for an anxiety attack. You'll face hundreds of possible directions, each so interrelated that it becomes difficult to discern where you are headed.

A Product Triad helps keep a balance in your decisions. As you confront the process of sorting out options, it's a discussion starter and creativity stimulator. You begin using the triad (shown in Figure 4-5) by imagining your product in the center of a triangle. In each corner are competitive opportunities to innovate, to improve quality, and to lower costs. In which corner do you decide to allocate your resources? Can you innovate product features? Can you find ways to make the product or deliver the service for less? Will improving the product quality improve sales? How could you improve quality? If the executives at your competition were looking at the same Product Triad, how would they plan and how would that affect you? Here's a scenario where a Product Triad was put to good use.

At a prestigious urban hotel, Tom, the general manager, has urged Russ, the food and beverage (F&B) manager, to improve the once robust Sunday brunch business. The general manager's frustration stems from the decline of the brunch as a profit center. In the past two years, it has fallen from 18 percent of the restaurant's income to 4 percent. Tom refuses to accept that other hotels outperform his own for this traditional weekend outing. He wants a plan from the F&B manager—now.

Behind the scenes, the F&B staff realize that they have been altering the brunch nearly every week at the insistence of the general manager, as he has tried to get his ideas into the meal. Now he wants a plan! Rather than submit a plan, Russ invites Tom to his staff meeting.

Russ [F&B manager]: Let's spend today's meeting on the Sunday brunch problem and what we can do about bringing it back up to where it was last year. I invited Tom to sit in with us. We're both concerned about our product, but we need some ideas about where to head. Do you want to add a comment, Tom?

Tom [general manager]: We're the premier hotel in town, and we should have the premier Sunday brunch—unusual, dramatic food presentation, superb quality and service—plus it's important to keep the price in line with the competition.

Joyce [assistant F&B manager]: One of the problems is that we shift priority every week. We run exotic themes, then shift back to simpler selections to reduce, our price. I think the public views us as inconsistent.

Jorge [executive chef]: We used to be known for brunches that were showstoppers, real occasions. I think that's what people want.

Tom: But the economy has softened weekend vacation travel. Businesspeople don't brunch on Sunday. We've got to get the locals in here, and they won't come if the price isn't competitive.

Russ: Can we use the Product Triad diagram that the corporate execs brought in? [*He points to the triad.*] Here we are in the center, not satisfied with our product. We have to pull something else into the center and we know that's difficult.

Pulling two things in is harder. Pulling three in is probably impossible. So what do we pull?

Joyce: It has to be quality. That's what we're known for.

Russ: But maybe we have enough quality here in the core from the spin-off we get from our four-star restaurants. Has anyone heard comments about needing more quality?

Tom: No, but we can't let quality slip.

Russ: We won't. The question is: Do we need to pull more quality into our product core?

Jorge: I see what you're saying. That's why we should concentrate on the innovation leg of the chart. We have the quality. We don't want to move to the low-cost path. We should innovate more.

Tom: I agree that we have to innovate. And it makes sense that we can't do that and play the price game, too.

Russ: Let's focus on innovating. Our objective will be to keep the quality at the level it is now but add a twist that will intrigue locals to come here Sunday mornings. What about a chocolate dessert bar?

*   *   *   *   *

What the food and beverage manager accomplished with a simple visual might have taken an enormous effort in written form, and probably with fewer results. Using a Product Triad to understand what your product core is and what needs to be pulled into the core for improvement is a simplifying technique that can put the entire group on the same wavelength.

Seeing the Big Picture: The Product Life Cycle

If you ever took a marketing course, you learned about product life cycles. Traditionally, the cycle breaks down into four phases: introduction, growth, maturity, and decline. Knowing where your product sits in the life cycle can boost understanding of its likely future and how to change that future.

In today's marketing environment, most product life

Figure 4-6. The Product Life Cycle.

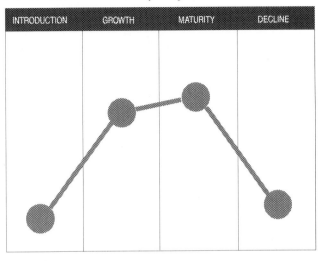

cycles are on fast spin. The market changes weekly for some products. Technological, economic, regulatory, and environmental concerns hit with alarmingly sudden impact. Products still have life cycles, but increasingly, these cycles look more like models of an atom than the simple curve we learned in textbooks.

We can build a visual model that can aid in deciding where your product is and where it can go. This model begins with the familiar Product Life Cycle shown in Figure 4-6. We can take the inevitability of this chart to heart, or we can begin to tinker with it. That tinkering can create provocative, unexpected, successful new product directions. Here's how a lawn treatment service successfully tinkered with a Product Life Cycle.

Chemblade, a regional lawn treatment service, provides seasonal maintenance for residential lawns. While this includes cutting and trimming, the company makes 85 percent of its income from applying fertilizers and pesticides. The application industry began to develop in the late 1950s and reached maturity in the 1980s, when the growth of new homes de-

Figure 4-7. Adding extensions onto the Product Life Cycle.

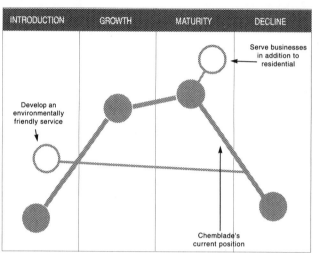

clined and the recession forced homeowners to reduce nonessential purchases. Heavy competition, price cutting, lack of innovation, and aggressive advertising programs characterize this mature product category just on the verge of decline.

You must make an honest appraisal of where you are in the Product Life Cycle to evaluate your options. Chemblade's industry has peaked in growth, moving to the far side of a mature product, and it can expect to decline in time.

Figure 4-7 shows where Chemblade is in the Product Life Cycle with an arrow. We can begin to modify the chart visually by coupling ideas and placement together. For example, Chemblade can add a possible new direction that will keep the company in the "Maturity" zone longer (meaning it keeps income high and can harvest profits). This new direction could represent service to businesses with lawns, which would add immediate volume and which Chemblade has the equipment and personnel to handle without added investment.

The company can also recognize that the market's needs might change the image of its product. Chemical applications may not be as acceptable to a more environmentally sensitive market. Can Chemblade adapt and renew by altering its basic service? If the company sees a decline ahead, it is easier to accept the risk of change. Perhaps the change can be significant enough to move Chemblade back to the "Introduction" stage of the life cycle. Adding extensions onto the Product Life Cycle allows you to maintain your current position longer or even move back to the beginning of the cycle.

*   *   *   *   *

There are many questions that suggest themselves when you take a visual approach to evaluating your product. If you are introducing a product, can it be cross-promoted with an established product to move you back from a traditional life cycle position? If you are in the growth stage of your product's life, can you find more inventive distribution channels to allow your growth to continue at an increased rate for a longer time? With a mature product, can you segment and niche to earn maximum profits and delay the inevitable product decline? And if your product reaches the end of its life, what can you do to pioneer a new beginning?

Taking a Family Portrait: The Price/Quality Matrix

Products do not exist all by themselves, especially with today's drive toward multiple brands and niche marketing. A common challenge requires evaluating your product or a potential new product within a complex and competitive environment where you may even see your own company's products as "competition." A Price/Quality Matrix helps visually clarify what can be an intimidating array of data.

The matrix is a simple box with quality, compared with the competition's, ranked low to high across the horizontal side. Price, again compared with the competi-

Figure 4-8. Finding your location on the Price/Quality Matrix.

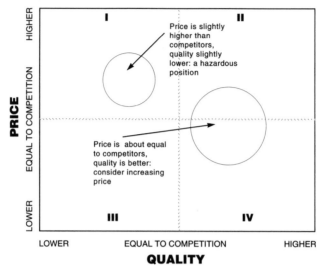

tion's, is ranked up the vertical side. The box is divided into four quadrants. Each quadrant has particular qualities, and your task is to place your products (and your competitor's, if you like) within the quadrants. Use a circle for each product, and let the circle size relate to the amount of sales earned by the product (see Figure 4-8).

What you look for are open areas in the Price/Quality Matrix where an opportunity might exist for a new product or a place to reposition existing products. You also look for overlaps, particularly among your own products, which might indicate some cannibalization. If your product falls in Quadrant IV, you should examine the potential for price increases. If you find your product in Quadrant I, you are highly vulnerable to competition. Here's a look at how the Price/Quality Matrix works.

Halo Golf is a well-established golf ball manufacturer. During the past five years, technological changes and competition

Figure 4-9. The Price/Quality Matrix for the manufacturer's four products.

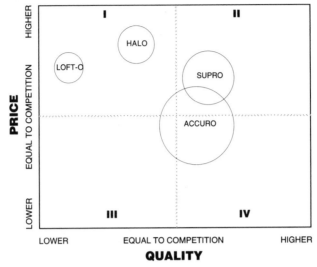

from the Far East have sent shock waves through the company. Halo made only two balls for more than fifty years: the original Halo and the Loft-O, which served the beginner's market. In the early 1980s, Halo introduced the Accuro ball, based on new materials and research. The ball enjoyed immediate success and is now Halo's best-selling product.

Two years ago, Halo introduced the Supro ball, which was positioned as a step up from the Accuro. Supro sales have not met anticipated levels, and management is considering the wisdom of introducing yet a fifth and sixth product. The Price/Quality Matrix shown in Figure 4-9 provides a visual guide to what the Halo management team faces. The managers used the chart to begin a product development meeting.

Alex: If this chart is right, and I guess we all agree that it's close, I worry that we have not been able to position our Supro ball far enough away from the Accuro to keep from cannibalizing sales.

Sondra: I think we need to work on that. We need to get a bigger gap between them in price. And we should have probably taken the agency's advice and not made Supro's package so similar to Accuro's.

Ted: Those problems are fixable. What else do you see here in the way of new ball introductions?

Sondra: We've been very fortunate to keep the sales level on the Loft-O. It's in Quadrant I—the dangerous quadrant. What if we introduced a new beginner's ball down in Quadrant III? Maybe we should consider dropping Loft-O's price and move it down there. At least we'd be in a position to sell a low-cost beginner's ball, and it might give us some nice volume.

Ted: Why don't you work on how to make that transition from a numbers point of view, and we'll consider it.

Alex: If the price of Accuro is really below the competition and quality is higher, could we raise its price?

Ted: We could, but right now it's our cash cow. I'm afraid to tamper. Let's talk about putting a new product up in Quadrant II in the far right corner and use that new polymer coating to make an ultrapremium ball.

Sondra: But we've never been outside of the amateur market. Can we really get the pros interested?

Ted: Maybe. But I think we might have a new breed of amateurs out there. Here's why. . . .

* * * * *

The Price/Quality Matrix brings into focus the reality of your product positioning, and also the opportunities available in the marketplace. With it, you can ensure that everyone on your planning team shares the same understanding and moves ahead in the same direction.

CHAPTER 5

Fish When the Fish Are Biting: Selecting Target Markets

Fishing. What other activity so perfectly matches the truths of marketing? First you decide where to fish. To do that, you put yourself into the mind of the elusive lunker, taking into account wind, weather, and possible feeding holes. Second, you decide when to fish. And if you're a real fisherman, that's not usually at a time convenient to you. Finally, you use the bait most suited to the palate of the kind of fish you want to catch. Fudge on any of these factors and you come home empty-handed. Good fishermen are inherently good marketers.

Who Changed the Rules?

To make a good catch these days, a new set of rules is emerging, yet most businesses still wait for them to become "official." The new rules demand marketing rather than selling, meeting customer needs rather than pushing products out the door. They involve speed and flexibility rather than size and power. The big guns like GM, IBM, and Sears have suffered as a result of these changing business rules. But many, many new businesses have flourished. In fact, small businesses (with fewer than 500 employees) now create over 60 percent of all new jobs in the United States.[1]

Business consultants, academics, and savvy CEOs know the new rules exist but struggle to define them. They need to look at three fundamental changes in our society that have left these business transformations in their wake. The first, globalization, grew from the explosion in communication technology and entertainment. We share more information than ever before, and it homogenizes our experiences, tastes, and ideas. The second change, computerization, provides the collection and utilization of data in nearly every facet of our lives—and certainly in nearly every business. In the early 1970s, it cost $7.14 to access a record in a database, compared with 1 cent today![2]

The third fundamental change, mass customization, resulted from the combination of globalization and computerization. Mass customization is the ability to incorporate an enormous range of options within a standard production and sales process. Customers want customized products and services. Marketing is the discipline of getting those wants identified and met. With the assistance of computers, we are moving closer and closer to being able to create customized products right off the assembly line.

Look back at the sales-driven company of the 1970s. You can visually depict how a sales-driven company looked by imagining any product. Then add prospective customers, and the task of a sales-driven company becomes persuading the customers that the product fits their needs. And since it doesn't fit the needs *exactly*, the most successful companies in a sales-driven world "make the most calls," "offer the best discount," and "are the most persuasive." Big companies that stamp out consistent, vanilla products—rather like a lemonade stand—must rely on a strong sales structure to create profits.

Now take a look at how mass customization upended the lemonade stand. With tools to reach people more selectively, and with computerized technology able to customize products, new and different approaches lead more directly to profitability. Quality, speed, creativity, flexibility, and service become core competencies for the new rules of business.

Using the Market Pyramid to Segment Your Market

Providing meaningful mass customization requires smart targeting. As you build your product to fit a specific market need, you inevitably make the same product less attractive to other market segments. The old answer was to build an average product and sell hard. Today, mass-customized marketers build an array of products by offering enhancements and features that are selectable by the consumer.

With limited resources, the problem becomes selecting those segments that will produce the greatest return. And, as many of America's dinosaur corporations are discovering, these segments add up to a whopping market that no longer must accept an average product.

Segmenting a market requires information, intuition, and imagination. No right answer exists in segmentation. You need to find a breakdown of the market based on hard data. You can obtain this demographic and psychographic data from your own customers, from published research, or from new research. But of all the ways to break down the market, you'll end up needing a good measure of intuition, placing your feel for the market into the process. Finally, segmentation means little without the imagination of how to use it to its fullest potential.

The company that can put together an accurate picture of its market and build consensus internally on how to approach each segment of that market has a significant tactical advantage. Many times in corporations, staff members work at cross-purposes because they do not share a common understanding of the marketing priorities.

Once again, a visual approach to the marketing issue of segmentation offers great advantages. With the Market Pyramid, you can build a picture of the segments in your business and rank the relative size and importance of each. Here's an example.

PedalMasters, a national retailer of bicycles and accessories, wants a more coordinated marketing effort. Currently, each franchised shop handles its own marketing. PedalMasters believes that economies of scale can give the local retailer marketing advantages that might not otherwise be available.

The management team, along with a select committee of key franchisees, began by looking at possible market segments. To aid the process, they used graphs to sort out possible segmentation viewpoints. With data from their own sales along with industry research, the team broke the market along several paths: size of purchase, time of year of purchase, age of customer, type of product bought, occupation of customer, type of retailer where bike was purchased, and frequency of purchase. This represented the hard data available. They assembled more than thirty graphs showing an array of information. For example, the average price paid by a customer rose, as expected, with age—until age 35. At that point, the average price paid actually began to decline. Of the thirty graphs, the team concentrated on just a few graphs that seemed to hold the most important data. Being able to scan this information visually aided the group in their segmentation.

The PedalMasters planning team used the assembled data to create a Market Pyramid representing their best approximation of the market. And while their pyramid grew from hard data, knowledge of the behavioral and social aspects of customers also went into its construction. Here's how.

First the group used industry data to distinguish the buyers of bicycles based on the purchase price of bikes, with the top-end bicycle costing over $500 and the low-end costing under $150. Customers naturally separated into groups. The first group, those who spent $500 and up, comprised just 3 percent

Figure 5-1. The basic data for a Market Pyramid.

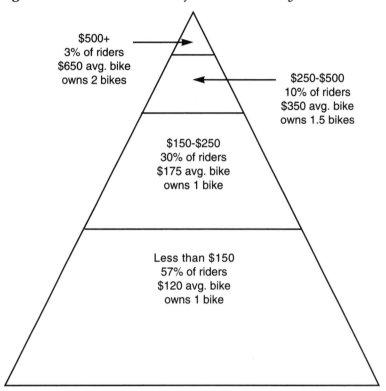

$500+
3% of riders
$650 avg. bike
owns 2 bikes

$250-$500
10% of riders
$350 avg. bike
owns 1.5 bikes

$150-$250
30% of riders
$175 avg. bike
owns 1 bike

Less than $150
57% of riders
$120 avg. bike
owns 1 bike

of all riders. The next group, in a price range of $250 to $500, represented 10 percent of riders. The third group spent between $150 and $250 and made up 30 percent of the market. The low-end group spent under $150 but accounted for 57 percent of all buyers. The PedalMasters team built a Market Pyramid based on this information, as shown in Figure 5-1.

As that pyramid indicates, the team was able to add more detail to these groups from the earlier research conducted. For example, they knew that the top-end buyer owns more than one bike. Defining each segment by level of interest seemed valuable. Research proved that low-end buyers rode less frequently. The team dubbed riders in this segment the "Infrequents." The group above them in the pyramid became the "Casuals." They rode regularly but were not "into" riding to the extent of the next group, the "Enthusiasts." This group

Figure 5-2. Adding segment names to the Market Pyramid.

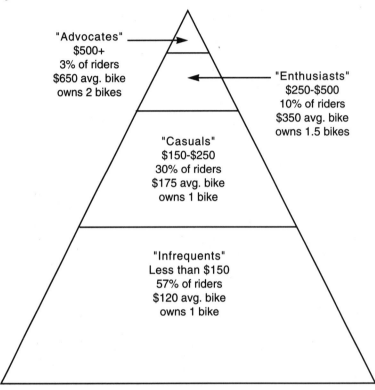

rode every week in season and often participated in social bike riding with family or friends.

Finally, at the top end, a small but influential group emerged whose members clearly were different from the Enthusiasts. This segment represented the most passionate cyclists, those who rode hundreds of miles a month and often owned different bikes for different purposes. Because cycling served as a major force in their lives and they were looked upon as the leaders of the cycling community, these buyers were called the "Advocates." And while they represented the buyers of only 3 percent of the bikes sold, they purchased the most expensive products and influenced many other riders in their selection of equipment or retailer. Figure 5-2 shows

PedalMasters' Market Pyramid with the segments named, which aids in recalling the different segments.

The PedalMasters planning team revised its Market Pyramid to reflect these new definitions and then took one more important step. After lengthy discussions about the relative merit of each market segment, they agreed to weigh their efforts toward each segment. They decided that the two groups getting the most attention should be the Advocates and the Casuals. The rationale for this decision rested on the importance of the Advocates as they influenced other riders. Without a close relationship with this small group, PedalMasters retailers would become "just another bike shop" in their communities and would find themselves selling more frequently on price. In addition, they would not dominate the service and accessories business that plays an important role in bringing potential buyers into the shops. Meanwhile, although the Casuals represented only 30 percent of all riders, they represented nearly all of the opportunity to sell upgrade bicycles. So the planning team decided to build marketing tactics aimed squarely at this important group.

The Enthusiasts certainly wouldn't be ignored, but the team saw that this group had already upgraded to a quality bicycle. Unless they became Advocates, there would not be significant revenue potential here.

As discussion of how (or why) to pursue the Infrequents developed, it became clear that two levels existed in this segment: (1) those riders who buy strictly on price and (2) those who weigh other issues. Given the nature of bike specialty retailing, chasing the price-only shopper seemed pointless with the discount store competition PedalMasters retailers face in most markets. The planning team would acquire further research to determine how this segment actually broke down and if there were enough Infrequents who shopped for more than price to justify a set of marketing tactics.

With the creation of a finished visual Market Pyramid (Figure 5-3)—in which relative focus on market segments is conveyed with shading—the management team of PedalMasters created a powerful tool to build its marketing plans and, more importantly, to explain the plan's value to PedalMasters retailers across the country.

Figure 5-3. The completed Market Pyramid.

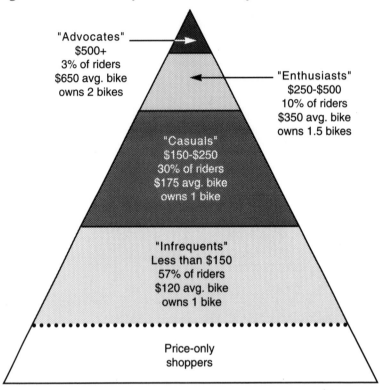

"Advocates"
$500+
3% of riders
$650 avg. bike
owns 2 bikes

"Enthusiasts"
$250-$500
10% of riders
$350 avg. bike
owns 1.5 bikes

"Casuals"
$150-$250
30% of riders
$175 avg. bike
owns 1 bike

"Infrequents"
Less than $150
57% of riders
$120 avg. bike
owns 1 bike

Price-only
shoppers

Understanding Your Place in the Food Chain

The promise of marketing lies in developing core competencies that meet the needs of customers. Sounds easy enough—except potential customers vary incredibly in their needs. Staying flexible to meet those varying needs can lead to real competitive advantage. Or real trouble.

The trouble begins when a business begins to lose perspective on its core competencies. Management doesn't understand its place in the food chain. This lack of focus shows up in two ways: (1) marketing to too small a customer (because it's easier) and (2) marketing to too large a customer (because it's attractive).

Marketing too small means that you bring a higher

level of core competency to the customer than it needs. Customers may seem to want these excess attributes— until they see the price. Then the reality of costs brings the imbalance of the company/customer match into focus. From the company's perspective, it faces the dilemma of losing the customer and all of the associated sales and learning-curve time, or else it must reduce the price and not charge for the company's core competencies. Most businesses presented with this dilemma choose not to bill the full value of their core competencies, using arguments about needing volume or getting a foot in the door for future increases. The simple fact remains that the customer does not need the company's level of competency. Marketing to the too-small customers erodes the company's core competencies, not to mention its bottom line.

But marketing too large holds trouble too. Chasing customers for whom your core competencies fall short of their needs can produce wonderfully optimistic projections but rarely much business. The real risk for the pursuing companies comes when they catch one of these oversized clients. The mismatch of skills becomes apparent and the account heads south, if the business is lucky. If not, the account grows out of proportion to the company, eventually dominating and dictating how it will be handled. Many businesses fail from this type of "success."

The first step in determining which customers are too small or too large is assessing your company's or product's core competencies. One tool is as simple as a Table of Skills (shown in Figure 5-4), used to evaluate the skills required in your business with a ranking from 1 to 10. (A 1 would indicate a serious deficiency; a 10 would indicate a stellar virtue.) Without an understanding of core competencies, you're doomed to drift into dangerous waters.

Next, find a method to break your market into a range.

Figure 5-4. Table of Skills.

T A B L E O F S K I L L S	
1= WEAK TO 10 = STRONG	
fast delivery	**8**

This can be based on something as simple as the prospect's gross revenue or as sophisticated as the number of units of product purchased. As the prospect size increases, you may find that you can market only your most specialized core competencies, ones in which you have a clear advantage over the competition and ones in which the prospect can clearly differentiate this advantage.

Then, use a code to assess your core competencies against the customer's needs.

1. A "greater than" sign (>) indicates that your skill level exceeds the client's need in a specific range. This makes it easier to convince the client to use your product or service but creates underutilized (excess) core competencies, which lead to lower profitability.
2. An equal sign (=) indicates that your company's

Figure 5-5. Symbols for evaluating competency by market segment.

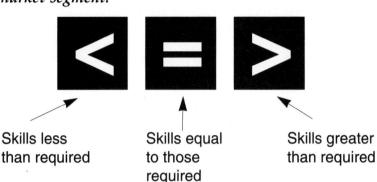

Skills less than required

Skills equal to those required

Skills greater than required

skills meet but do not exceed the customer's needs. This becomes your zone of optimal profitability.

3. A "less than" sign (<) means that your skill level is below that normally purchased by the customer. Often this means that the customer can find more-specialized core competencies to fill its needs more precisely.

With these three symbols (see Figure 5-5), you can plot out a ranking of relative strength, or a Food Chain, and create a plan of attack on target markets that will produce the greatest return. Let's look at how one advertising agency did this.

Spencer+Coho Advertising has just experienced its first year with no growth since its inception eight years ago. The four principals agree that something must be done, and while they can't agree on a solution, they agree that the solution rests on finding more business. The agency's reputation is built on its award-winning graphic design work. It boasts that it has the finest creative staff in the community, a growing city of 700,000.

The agency has an active business development committee

responsible for making more than twenty-two major new-business pitches last year and acquiring six new clients (a respectable 27+ percent "hit ratio"). But revenues from the new clients have not met projections, and with the normal client attrition, last year showed a slight decline in revenue.

The agency principals agree that cutting overhead (primarily staff) could have a negative impact on the company's high-quality work. With eighteen employees and second mortgages on the homes of each principal, the pressure has mounted to find a solution.

A recurring theme of the business development committee was a discussion of what type of client the agency should pursue. To a large extent, new-business leads fell into two groups: (1) clients that contacted the agency for a presentation as part of an organized search and (2) clients that the agency contacted because of the agency's interest in the account. All of the new clients the previous year fell into the first group.

Believing that they needed a fresh perspective, the agency principals hired a respected marketing consultant to spend a day planning with them. She opened the meeting with the following comments.

Consultant: You've asked me to work with you today on how to improve your marketing. To really do that, you're going to have to look at your company and your skills with brutal honesty. Otherwise, we'll end up this afternoon either frustrated or with a false sense of optimism. Since I don't know your industry well, you've got to police each other on the accuracy of what you say. As we move forward, I encourage you to correct and clarify each other so that we can build a group understanding of our skills and our place in the advertising agency Food Chain. Let's start by listing the core competencies of Spencer+Coho.

Frank: We lead with the quality of our creative work when we make presentations. It's our strength.

Consultant: Do most clients view creative work with as much sense of value?

Frank: I think so.

Margo: I don't agree. We sell that skill because we're good at it, but as our agency grew, we've taken on clients that want a more diverse set of skills, like marketing planning and support.

Dell: You've got to add industry expertise to the equation. If you don't know much about a client's industry, you're at a disadvantage against an agency that does. Then there's the traditional competencies that the client expects from its agency, like media buying and advertising creativity.

Consultant: What's the difference between advertising creativity and the creativity that Frank mentioned?

Frank: We're best known for our design work on image pieces like annual reports and brochures. Dell's talking about creating print and broadcast advertising. We're good at that as well, but it is viewed as different by clients.

Barbara: It seems to me that clients really can't understand the difference. Good creative is good creative.

Frank: What about public relations?

Dell: This is an area we've talked about adding staff in so we can be more full-service. But we're capable of doing PR now. We just don't get the opportunity.

Margo: If we were really good at it, wouldn't clients ask us to do it more?

Frank: But that's not what we're known for.

Dell: Don't we need to pay attention to what our clients need?

Frank: Which clients?

Margo: Let me use another example. We have the creative skills necessary to do direct-marketing work, and Dell and I have some experience working on direct marketing at previous agencies, but I think it's a stretch to say we're direct-marketing experts.

Frank: Who says we are?

Dell: You do, Frank! The presentation we did last week for Unitcom talked up our direct-marketing capability. But we don't have an in-house list broker, no database capability, and our creative staff can't even get the postal specs right half the time.

Frank: But Unitcom says they're looking for expertise in direct. Do you just want to walk away from prospects when we're trying desperately to get more? We do direct work for O'Boyle Auto.

Dell: But that's a car dealership, not a *Fortune* 500 company.

Consultant: One of the things I'm hearing here is that your competency level varies by type or size of client. That leads to miscommunication because each of you views skills from the point of view of your background or as they apply to the clients you work with. This would be a good time to get some of this down on the board. Let's list the core competencies you've mentioned. [*A list is produced.*] Now, how can we define the range of your prospect base? What are you looking for?

Barbara: A client that bills $10 million with us.

Margo: But realistically, we want a client with a $20,000 budget, too.

Consultant: Quite a range! Do they both use your service or competencies in the same way?

Dell: Exactly. None of the six new clients we added last year had budgets that would put them in our top ten accounts. And most aren't even spending up to their projected budget. The car dealership, for example, could care less about our great creative. The owner just wants the media bought effectively.

Margo: And we don't even place media for the few projects we've gotten from Unitcom.

Consultant: Could we build a range of prospects based on the size of their revenues and assume that companies of similar size will have similar advertising budgets and needs?

Frank: But there will be some exceptions.

Consultant: We can note those. Let's map this out in what I call a Food Chain.

At this point, the consultant listed core competencies vertically and the range of company sizes provided by the principals horizontally. She asked the group to agree on which of the three Food Chain symbols ($< = >$) belonged at each intersection. While there were some arguments and challenges, the task was soon completed resulting in the Food Chain Chart shown in Figure 5-6. Even before the chart was filled in, the principals began seeing a pattern that had not been observed before: Their most sought-after accounts were ones in which they possessed the lowest set of skills. It explained why they had not been successful in selling a full-service approach to large corporations despite their creative reputation and enthusiasm.

As they discussed the previous year's business development efforts, they noted that five of the six accounts acquired were in the under $10 million category, and the sixth was just barely a rung above. While they celebrated these successes with gusto, the net would mean six new clients for whom the agency was overstaffed and overskilled. Ironically, only one of the twenty-two business pitches made by the agency in the last year fell in the column where the fit would be most perfect: clients from $50 million to $100 million in size.

Why? As the consultant pointed out, the agency was reaching too far in its proactive pitches to clients that were too large. Should an account that size be retained, the agency would not have the skills in-house to handle it. At this level of the Food Chain, Spencer+Coho competed against national and even international agencies for the business—agencies with strong core competencies better suited to the prospective clients.

Because these proactive pitches to large corporations took so much of key management's time, most other new business was acquired through the "request for proposal" process. No RFP was turned away. And because clients tend to overhire, the agency was often included in RFPs for the smaller prospects and left out of the competition where they fit best. Spencer+Coho enjoyed a stunning success record at winning these small accounts, but now it was time to pay the piper. The accounts could not handle the agency's pricing, with considerable friction and a few sparks already in the air.

The principals at Spencer+Coho developed three targets based on this information and prioritized them. They decided to do the following:

Figure 5-6. The completed Food Chain Chart.

CORE COMPETENCIES	< $10 million	$10-50 million	$50-100 million	$100-500 million	> $500 million
Advertising creativity	⊃	⊃	⊜	⊜	⊂
Marketing planning	⊃	⊃	⊜	⊂	⊂
Media purchasing	⊃	⊃	⊃	⊂	⊂
Public relations	⊃	⊜	⊜	⊂	⊂
Graphic design	⊃	⊃	⊃	⊜	⊜
Direct marketing	⊃	⊜	⊂	⊂	⊂
Support services	⊃	⊃	⊜	⊜	⊂
Industry expertise	⊜	⊜	⊜	⊂	⊂

⊃ SKILLS IN EXCESS OF CLIENT NEEDS

⊜ SKILLS EQUAL TO CLIENT NEEDS

⊂ SKILLS BELOW CLIENT NEEDS

1. Proactively seek out clients in the $50 million to $100 million range and attempt to get on their RFP list.
2. Select a few prospects in the upper tier of size and then market only the agency's strength at that level: graphic design. This would be project work and not a full-scale agency relationship, but it would help keep the agency at peak creative levels.
3. Set a minimum size of client at $50 million unless special circumstances warrant otherwise. The business development committee as a whole would determine when those circumstances exist—the agency having special industry skills, for example, or a client poised for growth.

* * * * *

With the Food Chain, marketing planners can evaluate their company's relative strengths and then find the most reliable, profitable sources of new business. The process reduces the tendency to chase prospects who are too large and who might just eat you if you were to actually catch them!

Notes

1. *The Universal Almanac, 1993* (Kansas City, Mo.: Andrews and McMeel, 1992).
2. Stan Rapp and Tom Collins, *MaxiMarketing: The New Direction in Advertising, Promotion, and Marketing Strategy* (New York: New American Library, 1988).

CHAPTER 6

The Harmonic Convergence: Finding the Best Positioning for a Product

In the arrid mountains outside Taos, New Mexico, hundreds of people regularly gather to observe an event called the harmonic convergence. The event coincides with the celestial alignment of a certain group of heavenly bodies that believers suggest offer special blessings to those who are sensitive enough to care. Dentists, opera singers, retail store managers, and—I'm certain—a fair showing of marketing folks flock to these convergences, ready to believe that something out there puts order and control into their daily lives.

There seems also to be a harmonic convergence in positioning a product. Perhaps no other place in business do you find otherwise rational people who believe in mysterious forces than in the understanding and use of positioning as a marketing tool. Positioning appears as a supernatural gift bestowed on a product. It's not. Positioning grows from an environment of brilliant planning and management (or raw intuition and good luck). Books on positioning claim to provide methods to achieve it. They don't. Positioning includes an element of the supernatural that the best business plan cannot capture.

What makes the most sense to me as a marketing professional is a combination of both worlds. Use all of the tools at hand in strategic marketing, in tactical implementation, and in great management. Then hope that the stars line up just right.

Position as a Point of View

Position is a point of view. Unfortunately, it's not *your* point of view. Your product's position holds a fixed place in the mind of the customer. No matter how hard you want your position to change (or remain), massive forces are gathering to move it in the wrong direction. If you own a clear, firm, well-defined position, forces will attempt to segment your market and take the rich niches away from you. If you have a foggy (yet flexible) position, clearer forces will attempt to push you out of the way. Nothing's easy. Nothing's permanent. Your marketing decisions affect your position, but they don't create it. Believing you hold a position from *your* point of view leads to many product failures.

Position as a Place

If you own a position, you reside at a specific place. As you will see from the Gap Map visual tool later in this chapter, this specific place can be located as precisely as you can define the parameters and accurately gather customer information. Two issues come into play here. First, you might want your product to reside at a different "address," but you can't move without permission from your customers. That's why many new products are created. A new product enjoys greater mobility. If you see a greener pasture, a new product may be the easiest way to get there.

The second issue, place, means *one* place. You can't own two positions with the same product and the same customer. This remains number one on the list of marketing law violations. You can't be perceived as both the premium option and the economical choice. You can't be the largest and at the same time offer the most custom service. Even if you could, customers wouldn't believe you.

Position as an Arrangement

Like a yacht on an ocean cruise, your product's position is determined or fixed by its relative position to other objects. For yachts, these objects may be stars, islands, or buoys. For your product, they are likely to be it's price, competition, products in other related categories, or even packaging.

Knowing that your position will be fixed by the customer on the basis of many other pieces of information beyond the copy in your advertising becomes a competitive advantage. Smart marketers spend enormous efforts making sure the "sightings" taken on their product correspond to the position at which they want customers to see them.

Exploring Possibilities With a Gap Map

Most companies introducing a new product rely on marketing research to comfort their executives. When even small product introductions cost half a million dollars, we seem to need at least a six-inch deep pile of computer paper verifying the overwhelming need for the product. And when the product fails (as products do 85 percent of the time),[1] faulty research is still blamed. But is there any better way?

Yes—do the research. But go beyond collecting the pile of tables and statistics. With some preplanning, the research numbers you collect can be placed in visual tools called perceptual maps. A good example is a Gap Map, which compiles research data into a visual form suitable for planning discussions and creative brainstorming sessions. Here's how one manufacturer used a Gap Map.

Zia Chemical Corporation manufactures commercial cleaning products principally for the hospital market. Management wants to diversify into other markets to reduce dependence on health-care institutions. Zia's top-selling product is one of the best antibacterial cleaning solutions in the industry. The product is shipped in five-gallon dispenser bottles for dilution and use by hospital custodians. Zia's management recognizes that entering a new market will require modifications in product features and packaging. Six potential commercial and retail markets have been identified, and each of these markets now is under study. Key management and marketing staff gathered to hear a presentation from the marketing research organization that completed the initial study. Here's what the researcher told the Zia group.

> Our organization has completed the first phase of your research project, and I've asked for this meeting with you to present our preliminary findings. You asked us to look at six potential markets for the Zia cleaners. In each market segment, we identified a panel of one hundred cleaning solution purchasers and collected data in which the interviewees ranked features on two levels: (1) how important the feature is and (2) how satisfied they are with their current product. The data collected are substantial and have been assembled into a series of tables that you will find with the raw data in our report.
>
> But I wanted to provide you with a visual picture of our findings in what we call a Gap Map.[2] This is a perceptual mapping technique that is designed to show where opportunities for products might exist by averaging and recording interviewee responses on the map. Responses were ranked on a scale of 1 to 10 for level of perceived importance and for level of satisfaction with current brands. The items were then placed on a Gap Map. The Gap Map I am showing you now [*see Figure 6-1*] is for the home-cleaning service market. We know from our research that this market values products that leave no residue and are multipurpose, powerful, and environmentally friendly.
>
> The most important area of the Gap Map is the

Figure 6-1. The Gap Map for the home-cleaning service market.

IMPORTANT

(Best opportunity) ★Powerful ★Environmentally friendly ★Safe/gentle ★Price	★Leaves no residue ★Multipurpose ★Fresh scent ★Ready to use/no dilution
★Kills bacteria ★Easy-to-grip container	★Unbreakable bottle ★Hospital proven

DISSATISFIED (left axis)   **SATISFIED** (right axis)

NOT IMPORTANT

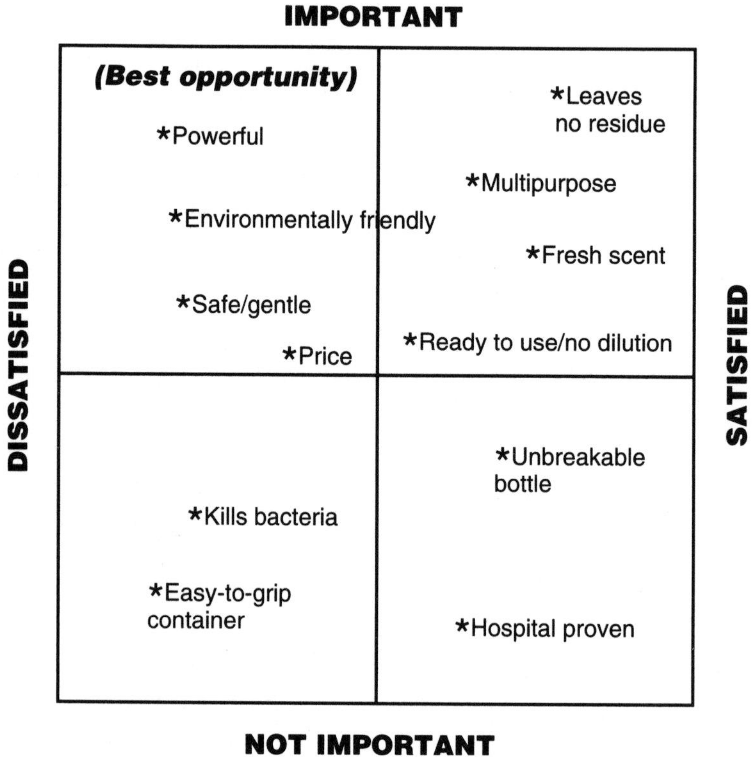

upper left corner, which holds the best opportunity for positioning a successful new product. It's clear that for the home-cleaning service market, creating a product that is both powerful and gentle to people as well as the environment can offer you a potential differentiation.

Based on our earlier discussions, you hoped that Zia's bacterial-killing qualities and hospital record would assist you in entering new markets. At least for this segment, we do not see those features as primary to a decision to switch brands to yours. But in another market segment, we did uncover a very different situation. . . .

*   *   *   *   *

Figure 6-2. Power Steps.

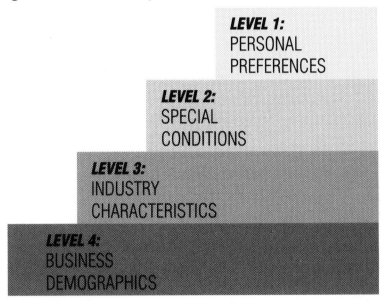

The Gap Map places features in a visual frame of reference. It assists in consensus building and shared understanding of the research collected. As you plan research for your next product introduction, ask the research organization to develop some form of perceptual mapping for you to use.

Getting There With Power Steps

Consumer marketing successes and failures get the headlines in most business publications despite the importance of business-to-business marketing. To help balance this out, let's take a look at a visual approach to how business markets can segment for better positioning.

Power Steps (see Figure 6-2) show the increasing levels of marketing power. They suggest that the closer you get to the top step (Level 1) in collecting and managing prospect data, the greater the chance of success in marketing and selling. The lowest platform of the Power Steps holds the traditional business demographic information that, as marketers, we are fond of gathering. This level of information is the easiest to find but does not hold a significant competitive advantage. Let's see how a manufacturer of digital cellular fax equipment used Power Steps in business-to-business marketing.

CellFax is looking for prospects for its new cellular fax. The staff began by looking at "Business Demographics," the Level 4 Power Step: the number of companies in CellFax's marketing area and their size, number of employees, and location. While this is valuable information, it is readily accessible to competitors.

Of more segmentation value is the Level 3 Power Step: "Industry Characteristics." This level of knowledge, beyond basic demographics, allows for the segmentation of companies within industries. For the cellular fax industry, such characteristics include the number of salespeople on the road for that particular type of company. With that information, CellFax has a real method of segmenting the market based on the assumption that these salespeople could use a cellular fax. The more salespeople on the road, the better the prospect.

An even higher level within the Power Steps holds "Special Conditions" (Level 2), which are the variances in how similar companies use products. These variables can change rapidly within even a single company. For example, CellFax's product has more potential in those companies that could benefit from but do not now have similar equipment. Once the purchase of cellular fax equipment is made, the Special Conditions change, lowering the possibility of a sale to that particular customer.

Finally, the ultimate power in positioning a product rests on the top of the Power Steps at Level 1: the buyer's "Personal Preferences." Is the buyer an innovator or a follower? Is the buyer decisive or a consensus-builder? What are the triggers that the buyer will react to most rapidly? Which combination of price, quality, and service will the buyer most favorably respond to?

By taking the time to walk their product up the Power Steps, the staff members at CellFax quickly learned what information gaps they had about how to position their product.

Talking the Talk With the Influencer Table

In many business situations, no one person is solely responsible for buying a product. While there may be a designated buyer, a group of influencers impact and often control the ultimate purchase decision. In these cases, talking to both buyers and influencers in a manner that is customized to their individual needs produces better results than providing the same information to all parties. An Influencer Table can help you figure out what to say to each party. Let's continue with the example of the digital cellular fax manufacturer.

CellFax's digital cellular fax machine has a number of important sales features that its staff was able to list. It:

- Provides high image quality resulting from a digital source and internal laser printer
- Is portable and durable as a result of solid-state electronics
- Is inexpensive to operate because the digital format uses less telephone time
- Maximizes the salesperson's time and speeds orders and paperwork
- Is less expensive than a laptop computer
- Provides two-way printed communication

In addition, the marketing staff identified four key influencer groups at prospective companies: sales managers, purchasing agents, controllers, and CEOs. With the above information, the staff began to build an Influencer Table.

To begin the table, each influencer type was placed across

Figure 6-3. The beginnings of the Influencer Table.

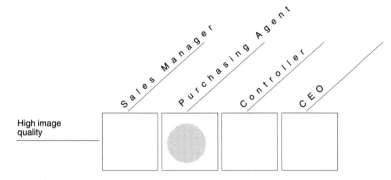

the top of the chart, as shown in Figure 6-3, and attributes or features were listed below. With research, experience in the market, and intuition, the staff was able to identify how important each attribute was to each influencer group. For example, based on research surveys, the staff knew that purchasing agents rank "high image quality" among the most important features they look for in buying cellular fax equipment (perhaps because of their collective experience buying copiers and printers). On the other hand, sales managers have little concern for image quality because now they are not even transmitting an image. Any image will be acceptable compared to the alternatives: phone conversations and the postal service.

Since some attributes are key to more than one influencer group, the staff marked as many of the boxes as necessary to form a visual picture of the market's areas of prime interest. They had to keep in mind that while all of the attributes may be valued by each influencer group, they were searching for the few, vital issues that truly have an impact on the acceptance of the product by the specific influencer.

With the completion of the Influencer Table (see Figure 6-4), the CellFax marketing team could set out to provide the best case possible to each buyer at the prospective company. In this situation, for example, the CEO would have two key areas of interest: (1) expense compared to laptops and (2) the ability to provide two-way communication. By zeroing in on presenting those issues to the CEO, CellFax improved its

Figure 6-4. The completed Influencer Table.

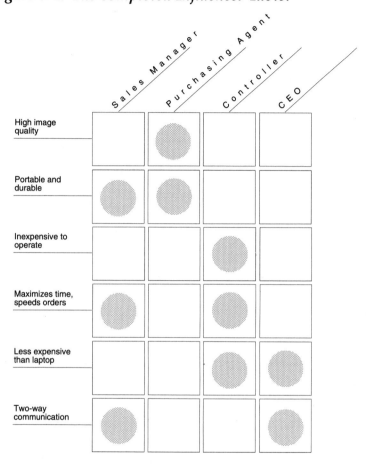

chance of a positive endorsement. Making the same type of pinpoint approach to the other influencer groups greatly would enhance the probability of a sale.

Finding Differentiation With the Positioning Cube

A product's positioning is fixed by each single customer, and that positioning can move based on what you do, what your competitors do, and even the customer's constantly shifting needs and desires. It takes a major

Figure 6-5. The Positioning Cube.

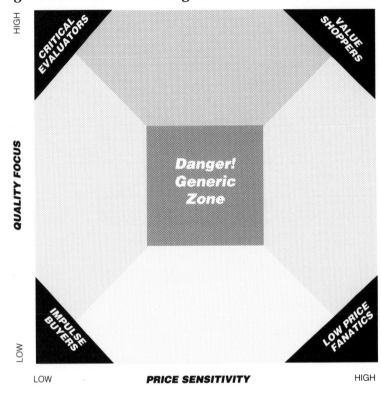

dose of ego to believe that you can control your product's positioning. But you can gently push it in a particular direction, and you can assure that your marketing decisions remain consistent with that overall direction.

Since positioning is created one customer at a time, we must group customers and make assumptions about them to have any hope of understanding the forces that shape your product's position. Customers vary on two vital scales: (1) how important quality is to them and (2) how important price is to them. In many industries there is room for dozens of competitors all providing variations of these two vital forces.

The importance of quality and price to customers can be shown with a Positioning Cube (see Figure 6-5). Customers who view quality as being of paramount importance and place a relatively low concern on price might be called "Critical Evaluators"; they are found in the upper left corner of the Positioning Cube. When customers place a high value on both quality and price, we can describe them as "Value Shoppers" and find them in the upper right corner. When customers have a high regard for neither quality nor price, they can be described as "Impulse Buyers." But with a high sensitivity to price, customers can become "Low Price Fanatics." Both of these customer groups live in the lower corners of the cube.

Differentiation takes place on the outer edges of the Positioning Cube. The center of the cube is dangerous territory where your product can become "gray" and generic. Ironically, the forces at work pushing you in toward this danger zone are often aided by product managers themselves. It appears that the middle zone would hold the most business. It seems that that's where you could be more things to more people, where you are less vulnerable to competitive strategy shifts. Wrong. To differentiate your product, you must be known for something and fix a place in the customer's mind. You can't do that in the generic center zone.

None of the outer edges of the Positioning Cube are inherently bad places to find yourself. For example, many highly profitable companies serve the Low Price Fanatics. But to stay highly profitable, these companies have learned to control costs and distribution and resist those forces pushing them toward a market looking for more quality.

With today's emphasis on quality, it may appear difficult to differentiate on a quality basis. But quality is relative. As successive product improvements raise the bar to jump over, someone among a group of competitors will always go a little higher. Someone will escape the generic zone.

Many companies that have earned a position with Value Shoppers have seen that position eroded by lowering their quality and price to try to capture a larger market share. They moved themselves right into the generic zone.

Companies that serve Impulse Buyers must combine stringent cost controls with promotional zeal. To begin improving quality (and raising prices) to grow their share of market, they will lose the features that made them successful and get sucked right into the generic zone.

The Positioning Cube offers a helpful tool for product planning sessions where each competitor can be plotted and positioning strategy can be analyzed. In Figure 6-6, a frozen pizza manufacturer plots the features of its marketplace and the relative position of its competitors.

Bert's Pizzas makes two products for the frozen grocery case market. Its Big Bert offers an extra-large size with premium topping and is positioned in the upper right zone of the Positioning Cube. Bert's aims this product at shoppers who look for value. Its second product, Bert's Best, is made in a more traditional size and sells at a lower price point. However, sales of Bert's Best have been plummeting while the Big Bert is doing well. The Positioning Cube shows why. Bert's Best falls in the generic center zone where fierce competition prevails with little product differentiation. The challenge for Bert's Pizza will be to keep its Big Bert well-positioned where it is now and to find a new tactic to move Bert's Best out of the center of the cube and into a more profitable niche.

Product Positioning vs. Service Positioning

Most of my clients give me a quizzical look when I say that positioning a product is no different from positioning a service. That's why this chapter tackles product positioning exclusively. One of the best descriptions of the difference, if there is one, is that product marketing fo-

Figure 6-6. The Positioning Cube for a frozen pizza manufacturer.

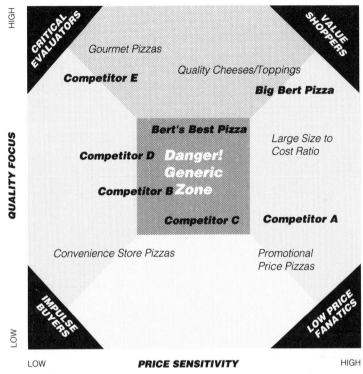

cuses prior to the sale while service marketing focuses after the sale. In today's service-minded product environment and with more competition now facing most service businesses, this definition is rapidly changing. The visual tools you'll find in Chapter 7's discussion of service positioning adapt well to product positioning issues.

Notes

1. Barry Feig, *The New Products Workshop: Hands-On Tools for Developing Winners* (New York: McGraw-Hill, 1993).
2. Information on market mapping was provided by Rick Flaspohler of the Kansas City, Mo.-based research firm Flaspohler Rose Marketing Services, Inc.

CHAPTER 7

![square icon]

If Ever There Was an Oxymoron: Service Positioning

The English language sometimes has a secret sense of humor. We can use combinations of words that just never should have been matched together. These oxymorons can be found hiding everywhere, quietly waiting for someone with a sense of humor to find and enjoy them. Oxymorons like *military intelligence* and *jumbo shrimp* find their way into stand-up comedy.

One of the newest oxymorons is *service positioning*. If positioning is the act of focusing, placing, limiting, and selecting, is this something we want to do to service? Great people and great companies emanate service from their core in such a way that they never need to concern themselves with how and when to offer service. It's just what they do naturally. But most service companies do not act as though they are in the service business. Browse in any good business bookstore and you'll notice that much of the writing today focuses on "quality" and "service." Look more closely and you'll see that the books on quality devote much of their efforts to the service arena. Even on the product side, you'll see that the days are quickly disappearing when the manufacturer that can get a good product out the back door at the lowest cost can prosper. Customers demand and expect a service component even from the most traditional product purchases.

Ironically, the service industry now lags behind many of the product industries in understanding and providing exceptional service. Too many years were spent expecting that the traditional service model would provide growth and profitability. But at the leading edge, tax preparers are now delivering your return to you, nanny services are offering round-the-clock emergency babysitting to regular clients, and hotels are providing not only room service and dry cleaning but personal computers with modems.

Differentiation vs. Just Different

Smart service-business executives know that not following the traditional model will produce better growth. You must be a leader, but take care to find real differentiation. That takes knowing what the customer wants and values. Is there significant benefit to the customer in the "different" service you plan to provide? Or is the service just different because you are trying to set it apart from the competition? Customers will quickly discard the "just different" and as quickly move their business to a service that provides a real benefit.

Another trap in differentiating your service comes when you focus on a customer need. There can be quite a gap between what customers may need and what they want and value. A fine line exists between visionary pioneers and stubborn egoists in the business world. To be successful in most service businesses, you must differentiate yourself from the competition. But take the time to examine if that difference is real and will be meaningful to your customers.

Finding a Service Position

Building a service marketing program without positioning is like building a bridge without math. A rare group of marketers and engineers could do their work based on instinct alone. They intuitively know what to do, in what order, and with what materials. The rest of us need reliable, tangible guides that assure us that when our work is complete, it doesn't come crashing down on us. The visual tools discussed in this chapter can help you position your services.

The Rule of 3

Despite all of the talk and posturing, few service businesses establish a clear, sustainable competitive advantage compared with those available to patented products or high-entry cost manufacturing operations. We usually find ourselves competing for clients. The client's selection process often seems subjective and mysterious. A quirk of human nature, which I call the Rule of 3, can assist you in visualizing how your service should be differentiated against the competition. The Rule of 3 simply states: *Clients find comfort comparing services in threes and will usually do what is comfortable.* I don't know why this is true, but in thousands of presentations for my companies and my clients, I have seen the Rule of 3 quietly at work. Perhaps you can put it to advantage.

To understand just how this selection process works, look at it from the client's initial point of view (see Figure 7-1). Clients enter the selection process for the purpose of comparing companies. They hope that comparison will provide a clear distinction among choices so that their task will be less risky, whether that risk is psychological or financial. Three seems to be the comfortable number to compare so that an extreme can be found on both ends and a selection can be made safely in the middle. Ironically, the less differentiation the client sees, the more service companies will be compared. The less differentiation in your industry, the more subjective and mysterious will be the selection process.

Clients will give someone the inside track and compare all other service providers against that competitor. This may be subtle and well-disguised by selection com-

Figure 7-1. The initial search for a service company from the client's point of view.

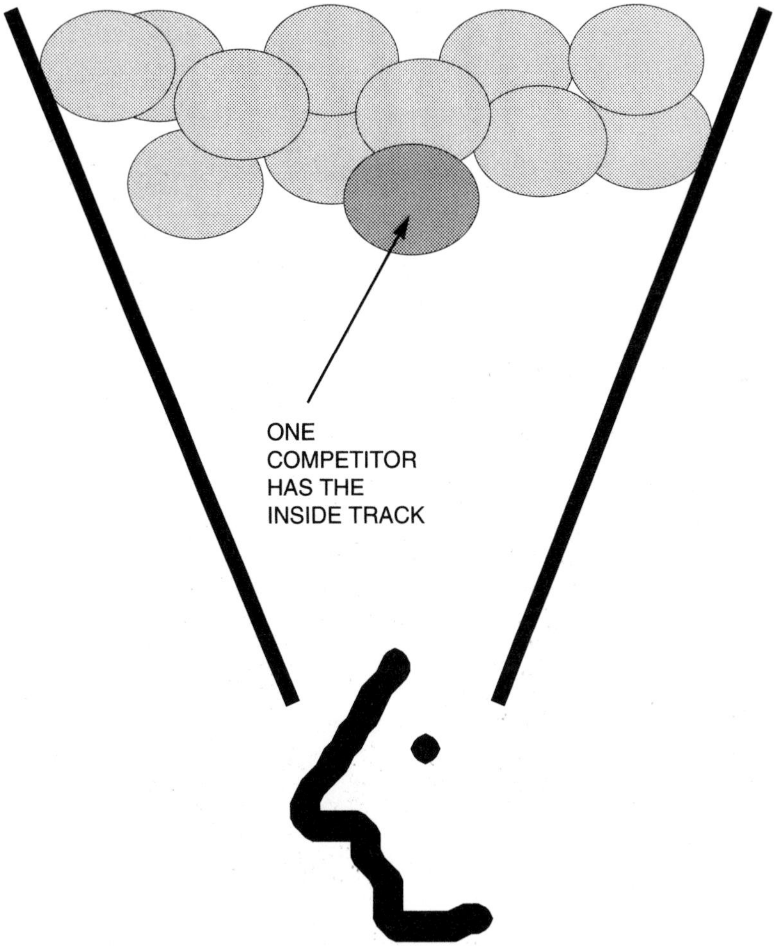

ONE
COMPETITOR
HAS THE
INSIDE TRACK

mittees and requests for proposals. No matter how fair it all seems, count on someone having the inside track.

Do postmortems of presentations and you'll see a recurring pattern. It's a pattern that can do you much good or much harm. Once you see it, you can often turn it to your advantage through positioning and differentiation.

The Rule of 3 allows you to look at the selection process from the client's point of reference and then to position your company to take advantage of that understanding. Let's look at how an architectural firm was able to use the Rule of 3 to win a contract.

Tower Architects and Engineers serves the northwestern states with three offices and fifty professionals. While its practice covers a wide range of projects, Tower has a concentration in designing schools, churches, and low-rise office buildings. Tower was asked by the school district of Tacoma, Washington, to submit a proposal for the design of a new school. Tower completed the proposal (taking seventy-five hours of nonbillable time) and submitted it to the school board by the deadline. After an anxious two-month wait for word of the outcome, the Tower partners finally received a letter saying thanks but no thanks.

Tower was caught by the Rule of 3 without knowing it. The rule suggests that the client will sort out competitors into three general groups. And when the client selects a panel of finalists, it will pick a representative company in each group rather than select three similar companies from one group. The rule defies logic, but from the client's point of reference, it provides three clear choices to make the final selection easier. Let's start the process all over again and look at how Tower might have won the contract by managing the Rule of 3.

The Tacoma school board had worked with a small group of architectural firms on the school district's previous buildings. New board members believed that a wider selection process was called for and invited thirty firms to submit requests for proposal. Tower Architects and Engineers did not know any of the board members and had not worked on any past Tacoma school district projects. The Rule of 3 would suggest that Tower might not want to spent the effort to submit a proposal unless the Tower partners believed they could differentiate in a way that got them to be one of three finalists. Tower believed it had qualifications that made it a good candidate for the Tacoma project and decided to submit a proposal. At this point, Tower wanted to move from the "Reviewed" status, with the twenty-nine other architectural firms submitting proposals, to the "Evaluated" status or select list (see Rule of 3 Chart, Figure 7-2).

The Tower partners got together to discuss the proposal and determined that they must break out of this pack by meeting some of the key Tacoma board members and showing special interest in the project. Tower suggested to several receptive board members that selecting a firm with school design expertise could prevent future problems, cost overruns, and potential liability.

At a closed school board session, all submissions were reviewed and a smaller group of nine was selected for consideration. This group represented three of the former school district architects, three new firms selected for their experience in school design (allowing Tower to make the cut), and three firms that the school district felt represented highly creative architectural styles.

The nine firms selected for consideration were asked to submit more detailed information. The Tower partners used the Rule of 3 to determine that to make the next cut to the Evaluated level, they would need to differentiate themselves from the three other architectural firms with school expertise. Looking at the total list of firms under consideration, Tower realized that several had been selected because of past associations, and one probably had the inside track. Several others had been selected for their creativity despite a lack of school experience.

Based on those firms being considered in this second round, the Tower partners suspected that the board was looking for a more creative approach to the new building project, while at the same time wanting the assurance of a firm that knew the practical issues of designing a school. Tower saw its positioning opportunity and built its final proposal around it: creativity and experience.

Of the nine firms being evaluated, a former school district architect appeared to be the front-runner for the project. This firm did competent work, and its managing partner had developed personal relationships with several of the longtime board members. Tower realized that the only way to dislodge

Figure 7-2. Contenders grouped according to the Rule of 3.

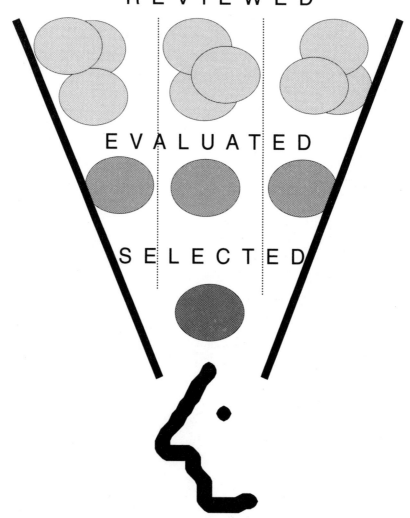

this front-runner was to develop interest among the board members in the creative merit of Tower's work. Thus, the final proposal submission emphasized Tower's imagination and creativity along with direct school design expertise.

The school board met once again to consider the candidates. Several of the new board members argued passionately for the need to set a high standard in the new school's architecture and to hire a firm with a sense of excitement and imagination. Other members reminded the board of its good relationship with, and the reliability of, the apparent front-runner. Three finalists emerged: the former architect and front-runner, a small but creative firm, and Tower. After much debate, Tower won the contract. Knowing how board members would group the competitors by assessing which firms they had selected for consideration tipped Tower off to the winning positioning. "Creativity with experience" provided the safest compromise position for a majority of the board and the winning formula for Tower Architects.

The Personality Quadrant

Like Tower Architects, many service organizations wait until a live prospect presents itself and then attempt to adjust to whatever positioning they believe the prospect wants. A more proactive approach to this positioning strategy predetermines the personality (psychographics) of the prospect segments and then devises tactics to appeal to each important segment.

A word of caution: Nearly every service organization attempts to do too much and, as a result, diffuses and weakens its position. The cult of customer service has increased this tendency by implying that the best companies go out of their way to do just about anything for a customer. Instead, you should pick the customers that fit you best and give them extraordinary service because you understand them. Then add more of *those* customers rather than expanding and diluting your organization's competencies with an entirely different style of customer.

A Personality Quadrant adds an element of fun to the positioning process. With this visual tool, you get the opportunity to place your clients and prospects by their psychographic characteristics rather than by traditional demographic means. But don't be deceived by its simplicity: It's a powerful tool for sharpening your service position. Here's how one service organization used it.

Office Partners, Inc., consults with businesses on space planning, interior design, ergonomic design, and office furniture selection. The three owners manage a staff of thirty design professionals. The company generates all of its income from fees rather than commissions on furniture sales and has built a reputation for objectivity and style. While the home base for Office Partners is Los Angeles, the owners want to move into new markets in California. The owners—J. J., Misha, and Doris—find themselves with a desire to expand but too many choices on just how to accomplish it.

Misha: We've all agreed that Office Partners has a distinctive presence in the market for our design style. That's what we're known for. If we expand, I hope we do more of the same rather than attempt to be something to everyone.

J. J.: I liked your idea last week of studying those clients we have been most successful with and then building on that.

Doris: There's so much work here in L.A. that opening an out-of-town office just doesn't make sense to me.

J. J.: Can we work through the chart that Misha brought last time?

Doris: If you think it will help.

Misha: To use this Personality Quadrant, we need to determine the attributes that are critical to our customer base. The work we did last week suggested that the key attributes are cost and size. Still agree?

J. J.: I still think that attitude about cost separates the customers very easily. But the more I think about size, the more I wonder if the real difference is style of company—whether it is a traditional corporation or more entrepreneurial.

Figure 7-3. The beginnings of the Personality Quadrant.

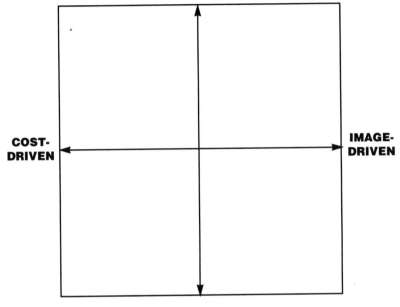

ENTREPRENEURIAL

COST-DRIVEN

IMAGE-DRIVEN

BUREAUCRATIC

Doris: The clients I love are the entrepreneurs. They want great style and will take some design chances. And they can make decisions.

Misha: Would it be better to describe the other key attribute as entrepreneurial versus bureaucratic?

J. J.: Sounds right to me.

[*Misha draws a large square on a flip chart and divides it into four quadrants. On the left side she writes "Cost-driven" and on the right she puts "Image-driven." At the top she writes "Entrepreneurial" and on the bottom, "Bureaucratic" (see Figure 7-3).*]

Misha: If this is our Personality Quadrant, what are each of the segments like and where are we getting our customers?

J. J.: The upper right is the preferred group because they really like innovative design and will spend money to get it.

Doris: But the larger companies that can pay us substantial design fees will be located in the lower right quadrant. Big companies with big budgets are usually bureaucratic. I can live with that if they will spend money on image.

Misha: What about the characteristics of the other quadrants?

Doris: To me the worst customers are the ones in the upper left quadrant. They're the ones that will pick your brain for ideas and then find someone less expensive to do the actual work. And it seems like the ones in the lower left corner that don't care about image and are highly cost-driven will be a low-bid kind of customer.

J. J.: I agree, but we've been bidding on a lot more work lately to try to grow the business.

Misha: Let's agree to call each of these quadrants something so that we can remember them later. What if we call the customers in the upper right quadrant "Status Seekers" since they want a lot of image and will pay for it?

Doris: We could call the ones in the opposite, lower left corner "Bidders" since they're looking for the lowest price regardless of style. It seems to me that the bureaucratic companies in the lower right corner that want high image work usually want to negotiate an agreement with a group of their executives. What if we call them "Negotiators"?

J. J.: Those upper left quadrant types really annoy me. We spend a lot of sales time with them and get very little work. How about calling them "Flirters"?

Misha: Looks great.

[*At this point, a Personality Quadrant has been built, as shown in Figure 7-4.*]

Misha: Can we use these customer personalities to help us think through our expansion plans?

J. J.: Back to the bidding thing. We never used to get business that way. I wonder if we're changing our positioning to try to get more volume?

Misha: What if we didn't participate in the bid market?

Doris: We'd have to do a better job of getting work from the

Figure 7-4. The completed Personality Quadrant.

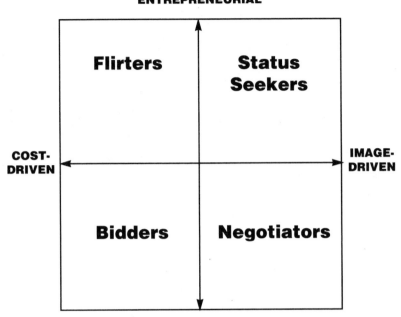

Negotiators. There just isn't enough high-level work from the Status Seekers quadrant in L.A.

Misha: I suspect that the bid work really hurts us because it doesn't use our relationship-building and referral skills. That's how we've built the business.

Doris: I could live without the bid process if we could get more work from the Negotiators quadrant.

J. J.: Seems like we all agree that we don't want the Flirters. Maybe we can find easy ways to screen them out early in the process. How would our approach be different if we spent more focus on the Negotiator types?

Doris: The Status Seekers want to see our awards and recognition and see that our work is on the cutting edge of style. I think our dramatic audiovisual presentation fits them perfectly. But the Negotiators want to see a process and methodology. They also want lots of references and credentials. We're not yet up to speed on that approach to clients.

Misha: Then the real issue may be whether there is enough work among Status Seekers in L.A., and if not, whether we should find Status Seekers somewhere else or expand more into the Negotiator zone here in L.A.

As a result of the planning session, the owners agreed to do more evaluation on the types of companies to be found in the Status Seekers and Negotiators quadrants and to build consensus on those questions before jumping into a new positioning direction.

*   *   *   *   *

If you skipped Chapter 6 on product positioning because you're in the service industry, take a few minutes and skim it now. In today's marketing environment, product and service marketing have so many issues in common that you may find the visual tools in Chapter 6 quite useful for your service-positioning needs. And if you're offended by the idea that service is like a product, wake up!

CHAPTER 8

Lizards, Sailboats, and Humble Pie:
Anticipating the Competition

With so many choices facing you in marketing your own products, it may be understandable why little effort is spent trying to plan the competitor's next move. But if you could anticipate the probable direction of your competitors, you might gain a real business advantage—or at least keep egg off your face. Take market leaders, for example.

Years ago, my son insisted on keeping a lizard as a pet. Many afternoons, a huddle of eight-year-old boys pressed their faces to its aquarium, hoping that Critter would decide to eat one of the dozens of live crickets hopping around the perimeter. Most afternoons, they were disappointed. Critter sat motionless, just waiting until he could catch his prey with the least effort.

The lizard's strategy parallels that of many market leaders. Wait. There's always plenty of prey. Pounce. Minimize effort. It's a strategy that works for fat lizards and a few fat market leaders.

Another type of market leader takes a more active approach. Friends who race sailboats talk in glowing terms about the strategy and tactics of the sport. And one of the tactics used applies as directly to market leaders as to the leader of the regatta. The lead boat becomes difficult or impossible to overtake when it mimics the course and tacks of its nearest competitor. With similar conditions, copying is a smart strategy. You do not extend your lead, but you do not lose it either. To pursue this strategy, you have to execute quickly and flawlessly. Many, if not most, market leaders follow this same strategy. If they do lose their lead, it comes from flaws in their execution.

Many companies hold on to market leadership with these strategies. A few companies even continue to earn their leadership role with innovation and productivity. But just as many market leaders get a large piece of humble pie served fresh from a young competitor that anticipates the leader's tactics and turns them into an advantage.

Picking Your Options With the Competitive Pyramid

The strategy of competition in marketing can be visually simplified to allow you to quickly see how competitors might think. You can look at the competitive field from their point of view. And you can make your plans to counter them.

A market can be segmented into three types of competitors and three types of actions they might take, as shown in the Competitive Pyramid (see Figure 8-1). The first type of competitor, the market leader, has the most choices—one advantage of being the leader. The leader can maintain the status quo (the lizard and the sailboat options), continue to enhance its product, or find niche markets.

The second type of competitor, the follower, has enough market share to make a run at the leader. In most industries, this is just two to five companies. The followers lose the option of maintaining the status quo. If they hope to overtake the leader, they must pursue a strategy of product enhancement or niche marketing.

The third type of competitor, the entrant, represents the start-ups and hangers-on who command only a small market share collectively. An entrant, even one ten years old, can pursue only one strategy successfully:

Figure 8-1. The Competitive Pyramid.

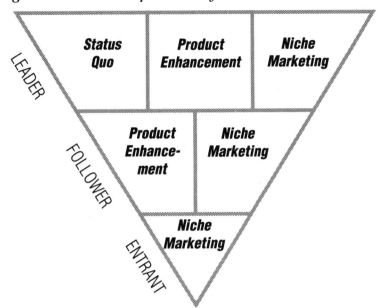

niche marketing. Ironically, many products fail because their managers worked on product enhancements not realizing that doing so was a dead-end strategy. For an entrant ever to overtake the leader, the entrant must change the product or category so much that the old rules no longer apply. Just what little Apple did to IBM in the 1970s.

Give your product and position an honest appraisal, and look at your options on a Competitive Pyramid. Put yourself in the place of your competitors, and think about their options. Get a group of your best thinkers together and try to anticipate your competitor's strategies. It's a smart way to grow your own business.

When You're the Market Leader: The Threat Box

Category leadership creates a bundle of benefits besides the obvious: more sales. The increased visibility and credibility provide a barrier that followers must break through. But to maintain category leadership, you must be ever vigilant. A visual tool that provides a marketing team with a simple technique for exposing potential risks to their leadership is the Threat Box. With the box, you identify all of those competitive worries that keep you well-stocked with Tums® and then apply a healthy dose of logic in viewing them. Here's a typical use of the Threat Box.

Tulip Diagnostics makes the leading heartworm test equipment for veterinary clinics, holding a 65 percent share of the market. The equipment is specially modified laboratory hardware that enables the vet to determine quickly if a pet has a potentially dangerous heartworm condition. Its eight other competitors split the rest of this category, with the closest at a 12 percent share. Five of these competitors are new entrants. Tulip's management sees the competition heating up over the next year and worries about maintaining the company's dominant position.

Over three successive early morning meetings, the management team and marketing staff met to deal with these nagging concerns about increased competition. They used the first day as a brainstorming session. The ground rules were: (1) Identify every conceivable threat from competitors that could happen in the next two years, (2) build on other people's ideas, and (3) express no negativity about any of the ideas proposed.

The team worked for two hours the first morning and identified a good number of concerns. These were listed on an evaluation form, which was copied and delivered to the team members later in the day. Each of the concerns was then ranked by individual team members on a scale of 1 to 10 by their probability of occurrence in the next two years and by their impact on sales (see Figure 8-2). This audit laid the basis for the actual Threat Box.

Over the evening, the product manager began to prepare a large Threat Box chart (see Figure 8-3). He combined information from all of the evaluation forms and averaged the team's

Figure 8-2. Taking an audit for the Threat Box.

	Probability of Occurrence		Impact on Sales	
	Low	High	Low	High
Vet focus on heartworm decreases	○○⊗○○○	○○○○	○○○○○○○⊗	○○
Competitor starts major ad program	○○○○○	○○○○○	○○○○○○	○○○○
Lose West Coast distributor	○○○○○	○○○○○	○○○○○○	○○○○
Competitor lowers price 50% below ours	○○○○○	○○○○○	○○○○○○	○○○○
Competitor lowers price 10% below ours	○○○○○	○○○○○	○○○○○○	○○○○
Alliance between competitor and drug company	○○○○○	○○○○○	○○○○○○	○○○○
Competitor offers free trial	○○○○○	○○○○○	○○○○○○	○○○○
Competitor equipment proves more accurate	○○⊗○○	○○○○○	○○○○○⊗○	○○○

response to each of the issues. At the team's meeting the next morning, the average number for each concern would be plotted on both scales of the Threat Box.

At the meeting, the product manager placed each concern on the chart as the group discussed it. "Lose West Coast distributor," for example, averaged an 8 on probability of occurrence and a 9 on impact on sales, moving it into the Level 1 threat zone.

Once the concerns were positioned on the chart, discussion followed about the relative placement of the issues, and a few

Figure 8-3. The beginnings of the Threat Box.

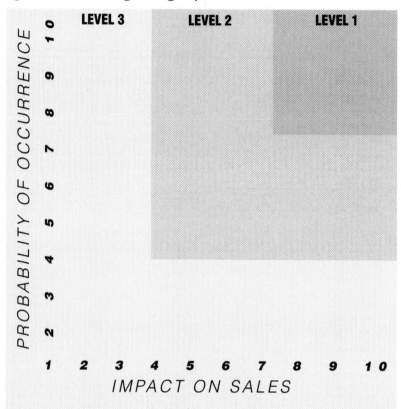

placements were changed. At the end of the second meeting, the team had a ranking of potential threats into three levels of concern. This is shown in the completed Threat Box in Figure 8-4.

On the third day of the work session, specific plans were developed to handle the one concern at Level 1 of the Threat Box, that of losing the West Coast distributor. Assignments were given to review the Level 2 concerns, and the group agreed to reconvene in a month to discuss how those would be handled. Level 3 concerns would be monitored by the product manager for any significant change.

As a team, the group determined what could most affect the company's leadership position and began to build contin-

Figure 8-4. The completed Threat Box.

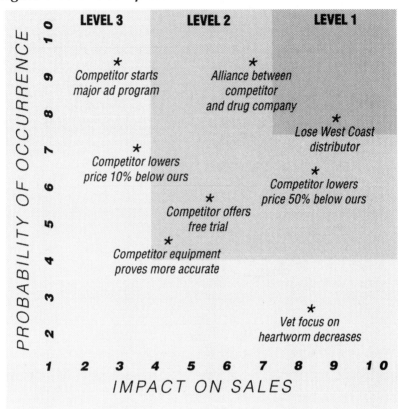

gency plans to deal with those threats. This approach ensured that the group shared the same understanding of the relative urgency of the threats so that an appropriate response would be made.

When You're a Follower: The Strength Grid

Followers have one valuable advantage: They have a target. Knowing what the leader's strengths and weaknesses are and weaving your strategy around them can offer enormous opportunities. But keep in mind that all of the other followers have the same advantage. You need to keep one eye on them, too. One way to plot this strategy visually and build an understanding of where the market players are positioned is to use a Strength Grid. With this visual tool, you identify the sales points for your industry and then rank yourself and your competitors on how strong each is on specific sales points. A Strength Grid provides an exceptional visual approach to seeing holes in your armor, or vulnerability in your competitors'. Here's an example of the Strength Grid at work.

Bristol Manufacturing makes an ultracompact washer/dryer combination targeted at apartment dwellers. Bristol ranks second in this market segment, with a 25 percent share, behind WashCo, which leads with a 45 percent share. Three other key competitors—NTI, Smyth-Dart, and Universal— split the remaining business.

Bristol's executive committee approved all marketing plans and expenditures. With a manufacturing orientation, this group was slow to take advantage of market opportunities. The marketing manager and her staff looked for a simple, clear tool to increase the executive committee members' appreciation of the marketing strategy battles and to earn their support.

To accomplish this, the marketing manager took a quick survey of the sales staff to determine the key objections or points of concern to the market. Eight items kept recurring: price, warranty, serviceability, capacity, reputation, dealer network, style/color, and model sizes. Next, she asked the executive committee members for a spot on their agenda to walk through Bristol's marketing situation for the ultracompact product.

At the meeting, she used a magnetic board to set up a Strength Grid by placing the competitors on the left side and the key selling issues across the top. Then she placed magnetic symbols in the "Price" column. When the company's position on price was a negative, she placed a − sign. When the position was a positive, she placed a + sign. When there appeared to be no competitive advantage or disadvantage,

Figure 8-5. The beginnings of the Strength Grid.

	Price	Warranty	Serviceability	Capacity	Reputation	Dealer Network	Style/Color	Model sizes
WashCo 45% market share	⊖							
Bristol 25% market share	⊕							
NTI 13% market share	●							
Smyth-Dart 10% market share	●							
Universal 7% market share	⊕							

she placed a solid marker. As the executive committee began to hear her presentation, the Strength Grid looked like the one shown in Figure 8-5.

The marketing manager explained to the committee that the sales and marketing staffs had reviewed Bristol's competition and had come to some consensus on their respective positions and the possible opportunities. She first discussed the price issue. WashCo, the market leader, had the highest prices. This was a competitive disadvantage for WashCo that was marked with a − sign. Bristol, on the other hand, offered lower prices than WashCo and about the same prices as Universal. Both had been marked with a + sign. Finally, NTI and Smyth-Dart fell into the midrange on pricing and got a neutral (solid) marking.

At this point, there was some discussion from the executive committee about competitors' pricing tactics, but in the end all agreed with her assessment. Next, she began the column on warranty by saying that Bristol offered the best warranty program among the five competitors. She walked through this column, explaining the positives and negatives for each

Figure 8-6. The completed Strength Grid.

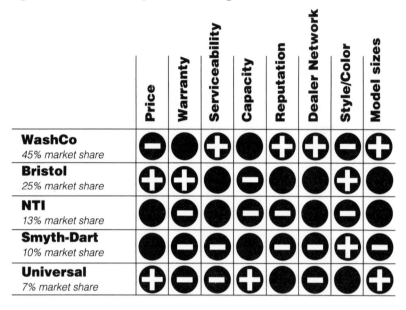

company. The same method was used for each of the columns in the Strength Grid. When completed (Figure 8-6), the entire group saw visually how Bristol matched up against the competition.

With that basis, the marketing manager proposed a series of ideas that took advantage of Bristol's strengths and of the competitors' weaknesses. She demonstrated these strategies by pointing out their rationale on the Strength Grid.

When You're an Entrant: The Entry Zone

In the ideal marketing world, you'd never choose to enter an existing category. You'd invent a new category! In a new category, you get to determine all of the rules, and best of all, you're the leader right from the start. But this is not an ideal world. As you develop a product and become an entrant in a category, you can save yourself from potential disaster by going back to the Product Life Cycle (Chapter 4) and thinking about just what the timing is for you and the industry.

Figure 8-7. The Entry Zone.

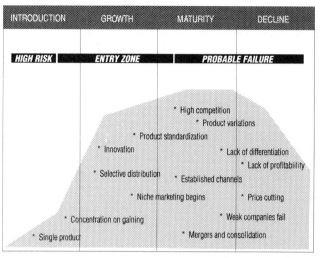

A modification of the Product Life Cycle, called an Entry Zone (see Figure 8-7), assists in thinking about and discussing this timing issue. Markets tend to exhibit distinct characteristics along the life cycle curve. For example, products in mature markets usually lack differentiation. You want to assess where you are by the market characteristics and how fast the life cycle is moving. Some industries (like dry cleaners) get happily stuck in the maturity phase for decades, while others shoot through the entire life cycle in a matter of years (for example, overnight delivery).

In the Entry Zone chart, you have three possible conditions. The "High Risk" condition comes with the territory in the early stages of an industry. Here, the key problem is not competitors but getting customers to understand and accept your product. Somewhere close to the end of the "High Risk" zone is the "Entry Zone." When timed perfectly, someone else proves the new market exists and you get in late enough to lower your risk and early enough to catch the growth curve up.

This zone gives way to the "Probable Failure" zone in

the early maturity stages of the life cycle. Ironically, that's when most new products are introduced to the market! In a fifty-year life cycle, plenty of time exists to plan your entry and exit strategies. But in a two-year life cycle, where many high-tech products find themselves, you move fast and smart or you're out of the game. By looking at the Entry Zone, you can locate the safest place to introduce a new product.

In Figure 8-7, the Product Life Cycle has been modified to highlight the three zones in which a product might be introduced. In the shaded area are common conditions that exist along each stage of the Product Life Cycle. You can gauge your product and identify which zone you are likely to be in. If it's the "High Risk" zone, your risk is high and so is your potential reward. The safest zone in which to introduce a product is the "Entry Zone," which corresponds closely with the traditional Growth phase of the Life Cycle. After that point, bringing a new product to market will often lead to failure.

CHAPTER 9

▓

It Isn't Rocket Science, It's Much Harder: Reviewing Your Marketing Budget

If you planned to build a rocket to send your corporate controller to the moon, you'd start with a room full of bright people and a straightforward problem. You could count on the laws of nature not changing. You could count on taking all of the time you needed. You could experiment and tinker until you got it right.

But if you try to build a marketing budget in the same way, your corporate controller will book *you* on a one-way flight to the moon! Building a marketing budget is not rocket science. Budgeting is harder. You can't count on the "laws" of the market staying the same. Competition and the business environment change daily. You have severe time limitations. If you take too much budgeting time, you end up with no time to complete your plan. And if you want to experiment and tinker, you may find a significant downside in research costs or see competitors getting the jump on you. The visual tools described in this chapter give you the ability to review your marketing budget, perhaps from a new perspective, but certainly more clearly and quickly.

The Budget Vortex: A Nonlinear Approach

Most companies make budgeting a process not because it should be but because it's too intimidating otherwise. The older the company, the more mature the industry, the more process. But marketing results come from

Figure 9-1. The Budget Vortex.

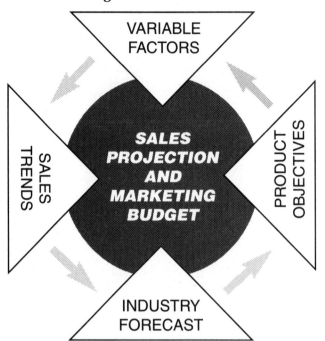

a complex web of interacting factors, not from a linear process. If your goal is only to beat last year's numbers by 4 percent, a process might work. But if you want to break away from the pack, you must think differently.

A Budget Vortex (see Figure 9-1) assists your budgeting team in understanding the issues that affect the eventual budget numbers and provides a gentle reminder of the interplay of those key issues. To arrive at a sales projection and a marketing budget, you must evaluate the four major groups of information shown in the vortex.

1. *Sales Trends.* This is where many companies start and end the budgeting process. In the vortex, it's a good place to start because it is the easiest factor to evaluate. What have sales trends been over the past three years?

What conditions had an impact on sales during the past year that may not be present in the coming year? Obviously, the best clue to next year's sales is last year's results. But that's just a clue. And in today's fast-changing markets, it becomes less and less valuable when used alone to plan a marketing budget.

2. *Industry Forecast.* This is the next most easily acquired piece of the puzzle for most companies. Taking a look at the trends in the industry should put your own product's sales trends in context. Is the industry mature and on the threshold of decline? Have your products kept pace with overall industry growth? If you've been gaining market share, how much more can you reasonably expect to gain? Building a marketing budget without a close look at what your industry is expected to do can lead to a budget disaster.

3. *Product Objectives.* These must also be considered. Product objectives can often be less tangible and more emotional, complicating an important assessment point in the budgeting process. Where do you fall in the product life cycle? What resources do you want to put into each product in your line? Is there consensus among the management team on what real expectations should be? Product objectives add a critical dimension to the plan.

4. *Variable Factors.* These are the most difficult of the Budget Vortex components to be attacked. They include productivity, potential price increases/decreases, and distribution changes as well as advertising and promotion. Variable factors represent points of internal control that can dramatically affect the marketing program and the revenue forecast. As variable factors change, they create change on the other sides of the Budget Vortex. A marketing strategy to lower prices to fend off a new competitor will impact product objectives. Losing a key distributor will impact sales trends. A trade association advertising program might alter the industry forecast.

Moving around and around the Budget Vortex with better and better information and reasoning will produce the most effective marketing budget.

Looking Reality in the Face With the Opportunity Gap

We hold market share in such high esteem in business that it sometimes blinds us to the reality of market conditions. Increasing revenues and strong market share in a declining industry catch many marketing budgeters off guard. The opportunity for growth comes only in the gap between your sales and the sales of the industry as a whole.

And "the industry" must be defined in terms of your direct competition. If you make real estate signs in a single community, you could view your industry as all of the real estate sign makers in that community. If your viewpoint becomes national or global and if your product line could expand from yard signs to street signs, you've certainly increased the opportunity. But have you lost touch with reality? You want to restrict your market definition to that arena in which you are capable of effectively, actively competing. Then you will be in a position to make a rational assessment of the opportunity available and the marketing budget appropriate to the opportunity.

Some businesses are so focused on volume or market share as a measure of their success that they spend little time considering the potential opportunity left in their market. This available potential can be called the Opportunity Gap. It's the difference between what you have now and what you could have at some point in the future. In the following scenario, a sausage manufacturer faces some challenges, which are clarified by the Opportunity Gap.

The new marketing director for Jill's Premium Sausage is worried about his CEO's high expectations in the marketing budget he inherited with his new job. Since the product was introduced seven years ago, sales and market share have really exploded. Since the CEO previously handled marketing, she took all of the credit for the company's success. And her revenue forecasts for the coming year project another large increase.

The marketing director is also worried about his initial market research. For the first time since Jill's was founded, the industry had a downturn in the past year. Despite that, the company's sales still grew at a sensational pace, with Jill's increasing its market share by 8 percent last year alone.

Now it was time for a reality check. The marketing director had his facts in hand and faced his first real challenge at his new company: convincing the CEO that while the party wasn't over, it would be seriously tapering off. It was a one-on-one meeting with just two simple charts and a lot at stake.

Director: Jill, I've been working on the marketing budget and have come to a few areas where I would value your advice.

CEO: Shoot.

Director: I've charted the sales volume for Jill's Premium Sausage for the past five years and combined that with the market share report we subscribe to. I call this chart [*see Figure 9-2*] the Opportunity Gap. Does this look right to you?

CEO: Sure does. I wonder if the industry total was really down last year or if there was just some reporting problem. Our sales were up nicely. What's this "Opportunity Gap"?

Director: It seems to me that we want to look at the opportunity available as one of the elements in determining a marketing budget. Five years ago, there was an enormous gap between our share of market and the total premium sausage sold in our markets. If we look at the industry sales over that time frame, it hasn't really grown much. But our share of market has increased from 11 percent to 68 percent.

Figure 9-2. The Opportunity Gap, looking back five years.

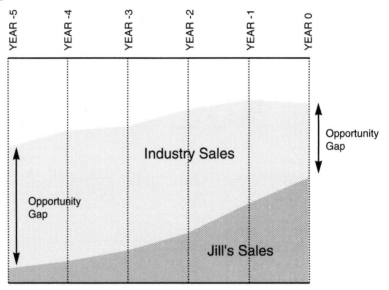

What this means is that the opportunity for growth is smaller now than it was five years ago.

CEO: There's always room to grow.

Director: I agree, and that's what I want some advice on. It appears to me that there is less room to grow in our current market than there was five years ago. That's because we have been very successful. I made another Opportunity Gap chart [*see Figure 9-3*] that looks ahead five years. In it I've shown the overall sausage industry declining based on what we hear from the market analysts. This curve also makes sense with what we know about our demographics and our customers' life-style today. I've shown our product projected to move from a 68 percent market share to 75 percent, but the net will still be lower volume.

CEO: I don't know if I believe that industry curve projection.

Director: No one knows what it will be. But everything we've looked at, along with the long-range planning work you and the board did last year, suggests a downward trend. If we build a marketing budget based on overall industry

Figure 9-3. The potential Opportunity Gap, looking ahead five years.

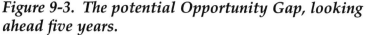
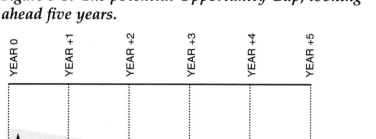

growth and it doesn't happen, we'll eat up all of the profits in marketing overkill.

CEO: It's probably safer to guess conservatively, I'd agree with that. Now look at your Opportunity Gap. There's just about zero opportunity left if this is the projection for the next five years.

Director: We still have opportunity to harvest profits from our strong market share. But you're right. We need to find a way to increase the opportunity available just as you did five years ago.

CEO: What about moving into a new market or taking a look at some new products?

Director: I think that would be the wise thing to do. Let's not give up on getting our profit out of the market share you've built up, but let's find a new source for growth. We need to do some reforecasting to bring our budget into line with this thinking.

CEO: And let's set up some way to get industry trends faster to see if our projections are too optimistic or too conservative.

With just two simple charts, the marketing director made a number of important points with the CEO, including a review of the unrealistic budget. Visual tools provide a common language that speeds up understanding and interaction. No matter what the future holds for Jill's, the marketing director has brought the CEO onto his team.

Evaluating Ad Budgets With Cost/Benefit Templates

Advertising, public relations, and promotional costs anchor most companies' marketing budgets, and yet their impact often remains obscure. This obscurity comes from a timing problem: Most advertising creates sales over a far longer term than the length of the ad budget. Of course, exceptions exist such as short-term direct marketing offers. For the most part, however, the advertising you buy in this year's budget will probably do more to help you next year.

Another thing obscuring the impact of advertising is the nature of your particular business. A few industries respond immediately to advertising. Some don't. But most fall into a confusing middle ground. If your business is one of those, your task in setting an ad budget is challenging.

Marketing managers create an array of formulas for how much they should spend on advertising. Some use an objective-and-task method in which each advertising task of the marketing plan is budgeted based on what will be required to ensure its completion. This method ignores the synergistic effect of advertising and often leads to overestimating the budget required. And in the end, it turns out to be an intuitive method anyway.

Some managers base their advertising budgets on competitive parity. If the category leader is spending x, they'll spend 80 percent of x. The fallacy of this method lies in the belief that one company's marketing goals are the same as another's. Then there are the old standbys: setting ad budgets as a percentage of sales or just simply what's affordable. While both of these common methods lack any logical basis, at least the affordability option requires an intuitive assessment of the market conditions.

Billions of dollars trade hands between advertisers and media. There must be an impact. Why, then, is budgeting so difficult, and why is the advertising budget one of the first to go in a downturn?

Building consensus among key management on the role of advertising can add rationality to an otherwise confusing, emotional, and frustrating part of your marketing planning process.

The marketing director for Jill's Premium Sausage scored some points with his visual tools in identifying marketing opportunities. He later used Cost/Benefit Templates to recommend altering the advertising budget. These templates provide the three common scenarios of how advertising expenditures will impact sales volume. Here's how the marketing director for Jill's handled his CEO on another sensitive issue: dramatically increasing the advertising budget.

Six months after initiating a marketing strategy for Jill's Premium Sausage in which the company determined to enter into a new product category, the marketing director needed to build consensus among members of the key management team on spending enough to jump-start the new product. The group had settled on introducing a fully cooked sausage biscuit sandwich to be marketed principally in convenience stores and grocery frozen food departments. Both markets were new for the company, which previously offered products only in the fresh meat case.

In previous discussions, the advertising budget for the new product was questioned by the CEO and CFO as far too high

Figure 9-4. A flat Cost/Benefit Template.

for such an unknown product. They pointed out to the marketing director that the proposed budget for the sausage biscuit was twice the level spent on their primary fresh sausage product last year.

As the marketing director moved into the budget part of his presentation to the management team, he used three Cost/Benefit Templates. These charts plot sales vertically and advertising expenditures horizontally. The purpose is to show the impact of advertising on sales. The first chart the marketing director displayed, Figure 9-4, showed a flat horizontal line for sales. The marketing director explained that it was his impression that this chart nearly matched the current state of the advertising-to-sales relationship of Jill's Premium Sausage. He reasoned that the company had earned a dominant

Figure 9-5. A Cost/Benefit Template showing a direct relationship between advertising and sales.

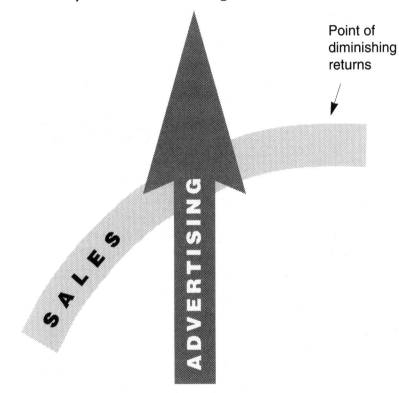

market share and that at this point, advertising dollars did not have an impact on sales.

To support his argument, the marketing director reviewed the advertising history of Jill's. Advertising represented 12 percent of sales during the first three years and now represented under 3 percent. Even though the total expenditure had not changed dramatically, the emphasis on and need for advertising had diminished. The management group generally agreed with those assumptions, and some members questioned whether the ad budget could be cut even further.

Next, the marketing director pulled out the second chart (Figure 9-5). This chart showed a direct relationship between advertising and sales. For every ad dollar spent, the company could expect to receive more sales. This relationship is enjoyed in few industries, however. The marketing director explained that for the new product introduction, it didn't seem logical to believe that for every dollar spent on advertising, there would be an increment of sales. In fact, he pointed out, few products enjoy this direct ad-to-sales benefit. Because the sausage biscuit was a new product and because it was in nontraditional marketing locations for Jill's, not all of the ad dollars would produce sales. The director pointed out on the chart that it seemed logical for greater and greater advertising expenditures eventually to produce diminishing returns at some point even in this best case scenario. That's where the sales curve flattens out at the top of the chart.

Finally, the marketing director pulled out the third chart (Figure 9-6). He explained that this was the type of curve Jill's was probably faced with. In this S curve, ad money spent at the front end creates little or no sales. After enough is spent to reach an awareness threshold, each dollar of advertising does create sales. You have to reach the threshold before any of the previous advertising has value. And, as in the template in Figure 9-5, there is a point of diminishing returns where more ad spending does not add to sales volume. The curve flattens out because the market has been saturated with advertising.

"I don't expect to ever get to that point," the marketing director said. "I'm just worried about getting to the point where the curve starts up." Everyone agreed with the marketing director that the third Cost/Benefit Template seemed right, but the amount of ad spending that would be required before the curve turned upward was still a confusing issue.

Over the next hour, a number of guesses were made on what this ad number might be, based on what other successful product introductions had cost, what money could be diverted from other promotions, and what "just seemed logical." To the marketing director's delight, the CEO came to the conclusion that the biggest risk the company faced was not reaching the advertising threshold. Anything spent to that point would be wasted if Jill's did not take advantage of moving up the curve.

Three simple visual tools had helped to clarify a confusing problem. Now, advertising expenditures would be visualized

Figure 9-6. A Cost/Benefit Template showing an initial investment in advertising, which is required before the advertising threshold is reached and sales begin to increase.

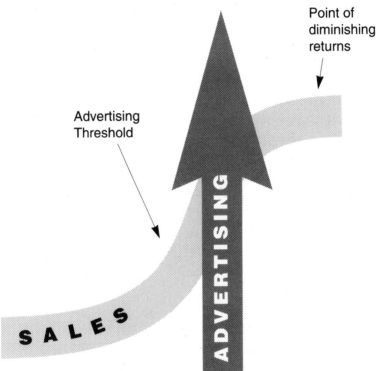

in the context of the charts and the threshold that must be reached. The marketing director assured the management team that his staff would work to get the threshold as low as possible by developing a smart media plan and attention-getting creative work. But everyone's expectations had been modified to accept the fact that the first volleys of advertising would be investments to gain access to the sales curve they wanted for their new product.

Budgeting Using a Lifetime Perspective

Boil down all of the interest in customer service and you find an increasing awareness of the lifetime value of a customer. But it's surprising how often this value gets overlooked in the budgeting process. Customers make up the real assets of businesses and yet are not valued anywhere on the balance sheet. But they can be valued in your marketing plans and budgets.

Creating customer histories and profiles from which you can readily extract vital information is the first step. This is most easily accomplished with a computer database program. In this database you can keep such seemingly trivial details as when customers first ordered from you, what style of product they most often choose, and which months they usually reorder. Then you can provide such relationship-builders as a thank-you note on the anniversary of their first order, a special announcement of a new product in the style you know they prefer, and a telemarketing call to simplify their regular reordering process. Even if you do not have a database of customer information, you can make assumptions about customer value that can later be enhanced and corrected.

Establishing the value of a customer can become a statistical maze. Companies with internal capabilities to do this use sophisticated models and complex mathematics. But there are easier ways. The Lifetime Perspective visual tool can be modified for your particular industry. To use this concept, you enter just three key variables— which I call years, margin, and actives—into a formula that provides a quick assessment of the lifetime value of a customer. The formula is given in Figure 9-7. Let's look at the Lifetime Perspective at work.

Link3 Cable Systems plans a significant promotional effort to increase its market share before new technology becomes available that will make competitive satellite dishes smaller and more affordable. Link3 reasons that once customers are hooked up to cable and satisfied with the service, they will

Figure 9-7. The Lifetime Perspective.

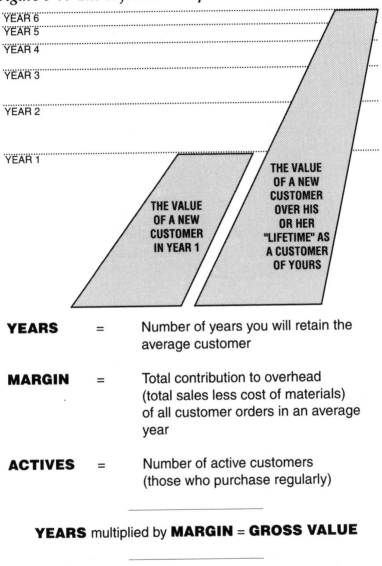

YEARS   =   Number of years you will retain the average customer

MARGIN   =   Total contribution to overhead (total sales less cost of materials) of all customer orders in an average year

ACTIVES   =   Number of active customers (those who purchase regularly)

YEARS multiplied by **MARGIN** = **GROSS VALUE**

GROSS VALUE divided by **ACTIVES** =
LIFETIME VALUE OF A CUSTOMER

be less likely to purchase the new dishes. The proposed marketing budget is three times greater than any previous year's, and to justify such massive spending Link3 must determine how much value will be generated from the promotion. To do this, Link3 executives realize that looking at lifetime value must be considered.

In a typical year, Link3 spends an average of $30 per customer on promotion. The company has 27,000 active customers. The new budget calls for an increase in spending to $100 per customer. To determine if that amount can be justified, the team at Link3 used the Lifetime Perspective formula.

The cable company reviewed its customer records and found that the average customer remains an active account for six and a-half years. Link3 generates $9 million in operating margin a year. By multiplying those two key numbers and dividing by the number of active customers, a lifetime customer value of approximately $2,167 was determined:

$$\text{Years} \times \text{Margin} = \text{Gross Value}$$
$$6\tfrac{1}{2} \times \$9{,}000{,}000 = \$58{,}500{,}000$$

$$\text{Gross Value} \div \text{Actives} = \text{Lifetime Value of a Customer}$$
$$\$58{,}500{,}000 \div 27{,}000 = \$2{,}166.67$$

The size of that number had a significant impact on how Link3 looked at its marketing budget and opportunities. It was clear that spending $100 to gain over $2,000 was a smart business decision. But it took looking at it from a Lifetime Perspective.

* * * * *

I've often noticed that in the budgeting process, highly creative people lose their innovative attitude—sometimes just when they need it most! By using visual tools such as the Budget Vortex, Opportunity Gap, Cost/Benefit Templates, and Lifetime Perspective, you can bring a fresh approach to the often laborious task of budgeting.

Chapter 10

The Joy of Fuzziness:
Forecasting Future Opportunities

American business yearns for simple answers—black and white with no gray in between, thank you! Will our new product be successful? Can we count on an open trading market in South America? Will the compact disc be replaced by the digital audiotape? Of course, the universe does not cooperate with American business's quest for simple answers. Which brings us to Lofti Zadeh.

At the University of California at Berkeley in the mid-1960s, Professor Zadeh invented "fuzzy logic."[1] In the world of computers, the professor realized, everything was on or off, yes or no, black or white. Shouldn't the computer work more like the human mind, which can see shades and make interpretations from imprecise, incomplete, "fuzzy" data? Unfortunately for Professor Zadeh, American companies and the academic community had no use for such irreverent thinking. After all, who wants fuzzy when you cherish black and white?

Enter the Japanese, who embraced Zadeh's fuzzy logic. It will usher in a tremendous wave of new products from Japan in the next decade. Already, Hitachi sells fuzzy vacuum cleaners that sense the amount of dust in the carpet and adjust the proper suction level. Matsushita now markets a fuzzy camcorder that distinguishes the jittering of your hand from the scene you are filming and adjusts to smooth out the picture. Fuzzy Japanese computers now understand and respond to normal human language. American companies are scrambling to catch up with what was originally an American invention.

Our penchant for black-and-white rules still lives in our business systems. As we work on annual business plans, we managers spend more time getting our budgets to fall precisely into the proper order than in looking at messy uncertainties and preparing for them. Worse yet, when we move to long-range plans, our need for precision often becomes so severe that we adopt a noncreative, nonintuitive planning system in an attempt to avoid dealing with the uncertainties.

We can learn something from the joy of fuzziness. Looking to the future must be an ongoing part of marketing planning. If we alter our requirements from black and white to allow shades of gray into the process, we'll enjoy a significant advantage over less fuzzy thinkers. We'll be prepared for however the future chooses to unfold.

Planning Multiple Futures: The Scenario Grid

Uncertainty: It's what keep most executives from taking long-range planning seriously. Yet it's the precise reason they should look at the long view of their products, markets, and industry. After all, the more uncertain something is, the less prepared you may be for unforeseen events. A number of tools exist to evaluate future uncertainty and prepare alternative plans. The most creative and intuitive tool is the use of scenarios.[2] The success of this process lies first in careful background study and then in the ability to suspend disbelief as potential scenarios of the future unfold. This planning tool tests your power of visualization. But to help that natural ability, you develop a framework called a Scenario Grid, which establishes the key variables of the problem to be studied along the range of possibilities for each variable. Let's look at an example using a Scenario Grid as well as another tool, the Scenario Process Chart.

Figure 10-1. The Scenario Process Chart.

High Plains Park operates one of the nation's oldest horse-racing tracks. The park, located on a reservation, is owned by a Native American tribe and is supervised by a board of governors. Prior to the annual planning meeting, a task force of board members gathered background information as a prelude to developing a strategic plan for the park. The sources of information were diverse, including a study of other track and gaming operations, interviews with futurists, analysis of historical data, surveys of key government leaders, and research on demographics and trends that might have an impact on the future of High Plains Park. The collected information was forwarded to all members of the strategic planning team prior to their meeting, as was the Scenario Process Chart shown in Figure 10-1.

At the beginning of the long-range planning meeting, discussion developed on the mission of the park as well as the objectives that were used to monitor the track's operation. In this first step of the process shown in Figure 10-1, some modification of the mission statement occurred as well as an enhancement of several objectives and policies regarding the nonbetting activities to be provided by the park.

In Step 2, the team agreed on a time horizon of seven years for the plan. No previous plan had been for more than three years, and a few in the group were uncomfortable with the long time frame. In the end, though, all agreed that a longer window would open up more uncertainties and perhaps expose slow-developing problems in time to adjust for them.

One of the most intriguing steps in the process (Step 3) involved a brief look back at High Plains Park for the same number of years as the team planned to look forward. This gave the group a sense of the amount of change that could take place in a seven-year time frame. And that change had been enormous. Several hours of intriguing discussions developed on what the park governors might have done differently if they had been able to look ahead seven years. Now they had the opportunity to do just that.

Then all of the background study paid off. As the group began Step 4, the team worked smoothly on what assumptions needed to be made about the future (such as regional demographics), what driving forces might exist (like the growth of high-tech communications), and what the greatest uncertainties were (for example, the level of tolerance of horse racing in a society with more and more animal rights activists). At the end of this first day of work, the exhausted team left the planning room with poster paper scribbled with dozens of notes and ideas covering the walls.

The next morning, the assumptions, driving forces, and uncertainties uncovered in Step 4 became the starting point for determining what major issues (variables) should be included in the plan. This information was distilled into a group of key variables (Step 5) most likely to have a significant impact on the park over the next seven years. Each variable needed to pass two filters: (1) how uncertain it was and (2) how much it could impact the park for better or worse. The group settled on four key variables: (1) new gambling competitors, (2) attitudes about animal rights, (3) offtrack betting, and (4) the growth of the West as a tourist destination. Then, in Step 6, each variable was examined for its most likely course (or mid-

Figure 10-2. The Scenario Grid.

	EXTREME	MID	EXTREME
NEW GAMBLING COMPETITORS	Government freezes gambling licenses	Competition remains about the same as current levels	Introduction of riverboat gambling and new track competitors
ATTITUDES ABOUT ANIMAL RIGHTS	Public interest remains at current levels	A gradual increase in concerns about horse racing	Strong opposition from rights groups to horse racing
OFF-TRACK BETTING	Government severely restricts offtrack betting	Interest in and licensing of offtrack betting stay at same levels	Significant growth in offtrack betting
GROWTH OF THE WEST AS A TOURIST DESTINATION	Tourism remains at the current level	Tourism increases by 50%	Tourism increases by 200%

dle ground) over the time period. Potential extremes were also developed for each variable as plausible paths that the future could take. A Scenario Grid developed that showed key variables, their middle grounds, and their extremes (see Figure 10-2).

To complete the second day of work, the group used a scenario-building process, Step 7, to examine a number of these potential realities. While no one can control these variables, the process of examining their potential impact could greatly assist High Plains Park in being prepared for a future far different from the one expected. Many futures can be built from the Scenario Grid. Any combination of the grid boxes creates a different scenario. The planning team discussed nearly a dozen combinations and wrote detailed scenarios on three quite different futures. For example, one scenario looked at the combination of what the world would be like with riverboat gambling and new competitive tracks, a gradual increase in animal rights concerns about horse racing, significant growth in offtrack betting, and a 50 percent increase in tourism. A description was written as if those events had happened and the writer were looking back seven years on how the park had been affected.

On the last day of the planning meeting, the group reached Step 8 and established strategies that could be pursued for various scenarios. And for each of the selected scenarios, signals were identified (Step 9) to indicate on which path the future might be unfolding.

At the beginning of the meeting, a vague fear existed among the planning team about potential future trends and their impact on the park. The visualization allowed by the Scenario Grid and Scenario Process Chart made these vague fears tangible and, once examined, even manageable.

Looking Ahead With Horizon Zones

As you think about the future of your markets, you may tend to view the possibilities on a narrow path. Usually the path goes from where you are now along a straight line toward growth. When marketing plans get written with these blinders on, you miss the opportunity to see other possible outcomes and to exploit them or, at a minimum, to protect yourself from them.

Horizon Zones provide a visual context in which a planning team can look at future courses. We visualize our current position in the center of a matrix and place possible outcomes along the perimeter. It can work like this:

Delta Toner and Ribbon provides businesses with printer and copier supplies as well as a fast-growing recharge service for depleted toner cartridges. Despite the economic downturn in Delta's market over the past few years, revenues have been

Figure 10-3. The Horizon Zone.

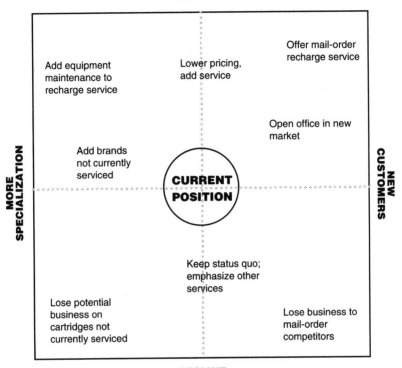

GROWTH

Add equipment
maintenance to
recharge service

Lower pricing,
add service

Offer mail-order
recharge service

Open office in new
market

MORE
SPECIALIZATION

Add brands
not currently
serviced

**CURRENT
POSITION**

NEW
CUSTOMERS

Keep status quo;
emphasize other
services

Lose potential
business on
cartridges not
currently serviced

Lose business to
mail-order
competitors

DECLINE

increasing 15 percent a year, primarily due to the growth of the recharge business.

However, a new competitor has entered the recharge market, and it appears to be gaining a foothold with a number of Delta's customers because it offers lower prices along with pickup and delivery service. Delta is concerned about the impact of the new competitor and is attempting to allocate its marketing resources to produce the most revenue.

It appears to the Delta marketing team that the new year will require a great deal of speed and flexibility on their part as they seek to preserve their profitable market niche. Using a Horizon Zone chart (see Figure 10-3) to form the basis for understanding and agreement on a plan, the group looked at four possibilities for Delta's recharge service: growth, decline, more specialization, and new customers. Situations were discussed that would move Delta from its current position to a future position.

For example, one of the group members suggested that without a change in pricing and service, Delta could anticipate a decline in revenue. Another saw the future of the recharge business becoming more and more specialized. Delta can recharge only one-third of the possible toner cartridges in use because the company does not have the necessary specialized equipment and inventory. Delta could put its resources into that area and still get a premium price for its service.

Delta's CEO asked if there were any ideas that could move the recharge business toward "New Customers" on the Horizon Zone. Several ideas surfaced, including starting a mail-order service focusing on smaller communities that do not have established toner supply specialists.

As the group members worked, they placed the possibilities on their Horizon Zone chart so that they could refer back to it as the meeting progressed. One conclusion became obvious: For Delta to continue to grow its recharge business, it must make changes in its marketing tactics. But no team member was certain how much change would be necessary, because the impact of Delta's new competitor could not be anticipated. With a general understanding of the future choices for Delta, the CEO asked his team to set some short-term targets and ways to monitor progress. At the same time, initial work would be done on moving their recharge business in a lateral direction, either to more specialization or to new customers or both. The team marked the direction on their Horizon Zone and agreed to meet monthly to look at the immediate course of their recharge business.

Delta's Horizon Zone chart (see Figure 10-4) provides an ongoing, tangible tool for getting everyone on the marketing team up-to-speed and making fast decisions. It anticipates that the team doesn't know exactly how the future will unfold but puts them in a position to respond quickly to changing conditions.

Getting to the Heart: The Critical Success Factor

An often overlooked secret of marketing planning holds that only a few of the strategies being pursued,

Figure 10-4. Planning "what ifs" on the Horizon Zone.

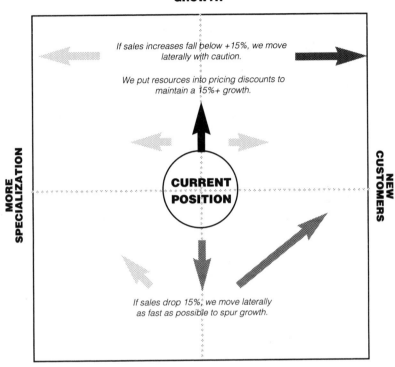

GROWTH

If sales increases fall below +15%, we move
laterally with caution.

We put resources into pricing discounts to
maintain a 15%+ growth.

MORE SPECIALIZATION

CURRENT POSITION

NEW CUSTOMERS

If sales drop 15%, we move laterally
as fast as possible to spur growth.

DECLINE

perhaps even just one, determine the success of the product or service. Deep at the core of every industry hides this Critical Success Factor (CSF)—a force so fundamental and obvious that it often gets overlooked.

The success stories we read always involve a person who locks in this factor and doesn't let go. Imagine how much more focused and forceful a marketing plan becomes when it is not burdened with an array of strategies that really are not necessary to success.

In fact, the attention and budget given to these remnant strategies sap energy from the strategy that contains the CSF. Unfortunately, finding your industry's CSF can be a real challenge. It's a matter of simplification. But simplifying to the wrong conclusion can be disastrous.

Figure 10-5. Focusing marketing energy.

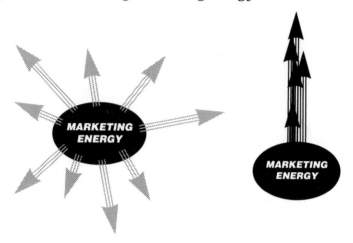

Even when the CSF is known, getting everyone to understand its power and to let it lead to a real competitive advantage requires constant effort. The brilliance we admire in the leader of a fast-growing company often is really his or her ability to simplify and then get others to commit themselves to that clear vision.

How would you describe the CSF in your industry? What one issue, if you managed it better than your competitors did, would lead to a significant advantage? Whatever it is, it's a safe bet that your fellow managers won't agree with you. In fact, that disagreement forms the hidden agenda for most business meetings, memos, and reports.

Compare the energy of most businesses to a light source. The rays of conventional light spread out in every direction. Sort of a nice warm glow. (Sound like any marketing plan you've been a part of?) But take the same energy and focus the rays in one direction and you have a laser (see Figure 10-5). Same energy, more power. It's no different in business. Most marketing plans try to do too much because the planners are not confident about where to focus their energy.

CSFs sometimes sound too simple. While "buy low, sell high" and "location, location, location" may be dismissed as platitudes, how many businesses have failed because their managers neglected to observe these obvious factors?

Does a CSF approach really work? Whatever they call it, successful marketers have a CSF. The chairman and mind behind Iams Pet Foods, Clay Mathile, has built a fortune on his CSF WHATEVER IS BEST FOR THE PET. No matter what the winds of fad are doing in his particular industry, Clay has instilled into all of his team the discipline of measuring every marketing strategy, tactic, and action by asking the question, Is it best for the pet? It's sometimes a tough discipline to follow, especially with increasing brand extensions and aggressive competitors. But Clay never wavers, and neither has Iams's growth or profitability.

A successful investment adviser explained to me that the CSF in her business was personal service, and the best opportunity to provide personal service came when a client faced an important life transition such as marriage, inheritance, divorce, sale of business, or retirement. While her marketing plan is informal, it never strays from her CSF.

The CEO of a half-billion-dollar toy retailer, when asked what the Critical Success Factor was in his industry, paused, grinned, and said, "Smiles." If his merchandise and service don't create smiles for children and their parents, his success will disappear. Every part of his marketing program is measured against creating smiles. And it works.

The CSF provides a powerful filter through which to view the potential strategies of your marketing plan. In the light of this filter, close examination and study will reveal how on-target the strategy is. The filter reveals

Figure 10-6. The Strategic Funnel.

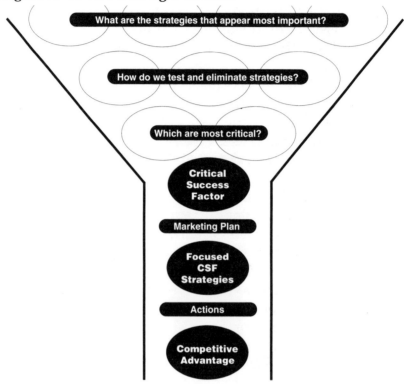

strategies that are defensive and exist in the plan to cover a lack of focus. And it allows resources to be transferred to the strategies that will most directly lead to success.

Building a Strategic Funnel

In the planning process, the Strategic Funnel (Figure 10-6) provides a visual tool for simplifying and focusing your efforts in search of your business's Critical Success Factor and ultimately a competitive advantage.

The team looking for a CSF starts by assembling all of the "suspects"—those issues that appear most important to the success of the industry. This is a time to get everything down that may be a possibility.

When the group begins to run dry of key issues, you

begin to evaluate and eliminate issues. One way to start is to ask two questions: (1) If we had clear superiority on this issue, would we dominate the market? and (2) Is this an issue that our best clients would say they value the most?

After the list funnels down into a smaller group of key issues, the team begins an intensive evaluation to find the most critical issue. Sometimes one issue clearly stands out. Sometimes there is a combination of several issues rephrased. And sometimes an entirely new idea emerges that is obvious as the Critical Success Factor.

Once the CSF is agreed upon, use it as a filter to evaluate all other planning decisions. At this point, the energy-depleting parts of the marketing plan become apparent and can be reduced or eliminated. And the "laser" part of the plan can be strengthened.

By using the CSF as a filter, a set of focused strategies should be developed that all tie back to enhancing the Critical Success Factor. From there, actions can be taken that lead to a competitive advantage. Over time, as your plan unfolds, looking back to your Critical Success Factor and then using it to steer decision making can provide your marketing staff with a more reliable method to make plan adjustments and to evaluate new opportunities. The CSF won't replace your marketing plan, but it can certainly give it a powerful head start.

Anticipating the Future

One of my consulting clients expressed a common complaint about long-range planning: Since we can't know the future with any certainty, it's really not worth the effort to plan too far ahead. And he's right in a way. If planning means locking in our actions and locking out our options, we should not put much effort into long-range planning. Inflexibility creates many business fatalities.

But if we can use the word *planning* to mean examining the uncertainties and possibilities that the future holds and anticipating how we will react to them, then planning's worth increases dramatically in value. It's never easy, but it yields results.

Notes

1. For an interesting perspective on Zadeh's work, see Daniel McNeill and Paul Freiberger, *Fuzzy Logic: The Discovery of a Revolutionary Computer Technology and How It Is Changing Our World* (New York: Simon & Schuster, 1993).
2. See Peter Schwartz, *The Art of the Long View: Planning for the Future in an Uncertain World* (New York: Doubleday Currency, 1991). I give copies of this clear, insightful book to all of my long-range planning clients.

Bibliography

Allio, Robert J. *The Practical Strategist.* New York: Harper & Row, 1988.

Arnold, David. *The Handbook of Brand Management.* Reading, Mass.: Addison-Wesley, 1992.

Berrigan, John, and Carl Finkbeiner. *Segmentation Marketing: New Methods for Capturing Business Markets.* New York: HarperBusiness, 1992.

Berry, Leonard L., and A. Parasuraman. *Marketing Services: Competing Through Quality.* New York: Free Press, 1991.

Clancy, Kevin J., and Robert S. Shulman. *The Marketing Revolution: A Radical Manifesto for Dominating the Marketplace.* New York: HarperBusiness, 1991.

Feig, Barry. *The New Products Workshop: Hands-On Tools for Developing Winners.* New York: McGraw-Hill, 1993.

Hayden, Catherine. *The Handbook of Strategic Expertise.* New York: Free Press, 1986.

Lele, Miland M. *Creating Strategic Leverage.* New York: Wiley, 1992.

Levitt, Theodore. *The Marketing Imagination.* New York: Free Press, 1986.

Linneman, Robert E., and John L. Stanton, Jr. *Making Niche Marketing Work: How to Grow Bigger by Acting Smaller.* New York: McGraw-Hill, 1991.

Lodish, Leonard M. *The Advertising & Promotion Challenge: Vaguely Right or Precisely Wrong?* New York: Oxford, 1986.

Magrath, Allan J. *The 6 Imperatives of Marketing: Lessons From the World's Best Companies.* New York: AMACOM, 1992.

McKay, Edward S. *The Marketing Mystique,* rev. ed. New York: AMACOM, 1993.

McNeill, Daniel, and Paul Freiberger. *Fuzzy Logic: The Discovery of a Revolutionary Computer Technology and How It Is Changing Our World.* New York: Simon & Schuster, 1993.

Michalko, Michael. *Thinkertoys: A Handbook of Business Creativity for the '90's.* Berkeley, Calif.: Ten Speed Press, 1991.

Rapp, Stan, and Tom Collins. *MaxiMarketing: The New Direction in Advertising, Promotion, and Marketing Strategy.* New York: New American Library, 1988.

Ray, Michael, and Rochelle Myers. *Creativity in Business.* Garden City, N.J.: Doubleday, 1986.

Ries, Al, and Jack Trout. *The 22 Immutable Laws of Marketing: Violate Them at Your Own Risk!* New York: HarperBusiness, 1993.

Schwartz, Peter. *The Art of the Long View: Planning for the Future in an Uncertain World.* New York: Doubleday Currency, 1991.

Sherlock, Paul. *Rethinking Business to Business Marketing.* New York: Free Press, 1991.

Vavra, Terry G. *Aftermarketing: How to Keep Customers for Life Through Relationship Marketing.* Homewood, Ill.: Business One Irwin, 1992.

Willett, George. *A Whack on the Side of the Head: How You Can Be More Creative.* New York: Warner, 1990.

Wilson, Aubrey. *New Directions in Marketing: Business-to-Business Strategies for the 1990's.* Lincolnwood, Ill.: NTC Business Books, 1992.

Index